IMAGES
IN
ACTION

IMAGES
IN
ACTION
▼▼▼

A Guide to Using
Women's Film and Video

Ferne Cristall and Barbara Emanuel

between the lines

© 1986 Between The Lines

Published by Between The Lines
            229 College Street,
            Toronto, Ontario
            M5T 1R4   Canada

Typeset by Dumont Press Graphix, Kitchener, Ontario

Designed by Susan Sturman

Illustrations by Gail Geltner

Printed in Canada

Between The Lines receives financial assistance from the Canada Council and the Ontario Arts Council.

The publication of this book was made possible through the financial assistance of the Secretary of State Women's Program.

Between The Lines is a joint project of Dumont Press Graphix, Kitchener, and the Development Education Centre, Toronto.

The excerpt of the poem on page 72 is from Adrienne Rich, *A Wild Patience Has Taken Me This Far, Poems 1978 - 1981,* (New York: W.W. Norton & Company).

Canadian Cataloguing in Publication Data

Cristall, Ferne.
   Images in action: a guide to using women's films and videos

Bibliography: p. 119
Filmography: p. 107
ISBN 0-919946-68-2 (bound). - ISBN 0-919946-69-0 (pbk.)

1. Feminism and motion pictures.   2. Feminist motion pictures.   I. Emanuel, Barbara, 1954-   . II. Title.

PN1995.9.W6C74 1986   791.43'0236   C86-094219-8

Contents

To Jonah and Kyle

Acknowledgements

Many people helped us produce this guidebook during the past couple of years. We asked several representatives from local and national women's organizations who used films in their own work to join us in developing the content. Their input was invaluable, especially in the "Small Group Screening" section, where their combined film use experience and knowledge of women's issues continually reminded us that one of the most important reasons for using women's films is to take a close, critical look at these issues. The women who spent many hot summer afternoons with us, and whose enthusiasm pushed us to continue, were Sandi Primeau, Penni Richmond, Frances Rooney, Margaret Smith, Barbara Waisberg, and Elisse Zack.

Our co-workers at DEC Films picked up a good portion of our workloads, which allowed us to work on the project, and they also contributed significantly to the book. Margaret Watson helped with the administration and legwork, and had clear insights into and ideas for the budgets in the "Organizing Public Showings" section. Jonathan Forbes added important detail to that section. Peter Steven provided us with challenging articles to read on feminist filmmaking, and critiqued that chapter in its various drafts, offering commentary and support. Other members of the DEC collective who gave time, thoughtful responses, and editorial suggestions are Debbie Field, Dinah Forbes, Marie Lorenzo, Lorna Weir, and Richard Fung.

Joy Johnson, who organized film workshops with women's groups across the country for Studio D of the National Film Board, offered both written reports and her astute personal insights. Renée Baert assisted in pointing out some of the unique attributes of women's video. Susan Ditta wrote the section "Not So Trivial Pursuits," adding important information on women's participation in film history. She also had many creative suggestions for the rest of the book. We wish to thank all of these people.

We gratefully acknowledge the financial support for this project from the Women's Program of the Secretary of State and would especially like to thank Eliane Potvin, Tamara Levine, and Louise Dufresne for their confidence in us.

Many women talked to us about their experiences using women's films. Others read drafts and made comments that pushed us to be more clear and thorough. We thank Margaret Cooper, Margaret Hancock, Pauline Head, Brenda Longfellow, Margie Macdonald, Beth McAuley, Arlene Moscovitch, and Abigail Norman. We would also like to thank Gerald Pratley and Sherie Brethour of the Ontario Film Institute for all their help and patience.

We would especially like to thank our initial editor, Frances Rooney, who edited the manuscript in its first draft stage. Her sense of humour and constant support of the project were indispensable. Marg Anne Morrison and Robert Clarke of Between The Lines made important editorial changes and pulled the book into its final shape. Their skill at clarifying our writing and presentation was invaluable. Our designer Susan Sturman and illustrator Gail Geltner made the book both attractive and more accessible for its users. We also wish to thank the women workers at Dumont Press Graphix who did the typesetting.

Throughout this book we have quoted from many women's experiences in using film. Most of these quotes were gathered from workshops, interviews, and informal discussions. We have taken the liberty of editing the comments to make them more concise and succinct, but we hope they remain true to the original. We gratefully acknowledge the ideas and creativity of all the women who contributed their knowledge and ideas.

Lastly, we would like to thank all women in Canada and elsewhere who influenced and inspired us to embark on this project.

More and more women today are developing, writing, and directing films and videos. More and more women are watching them, in theatres and auditoriums, community halls and church basements. And more and more women are using them to organize for social change.

The issues treated in these films and videos are as diverse and open-ended as the interests of the women's movement as a whole. Women media producers are exposing the extent of violence against women, through battering and rape. They look at women's isolation in the home. They argue for control over our bodies in matters of birth control, childbearing and rearing, and sexuality. They look at the successes too: women's contribution to history and the arts, participation in labour organizing, and role within the family.

A whole range of people — from educators to community organizers to political activists and unionists — are concerned about presenting such films effectively to their particular audiences and constituencies. They might be using film to educate or provide information on a special issue or set of issues, or to build support for a new organization, coalition, or cause. They might be trying to develop

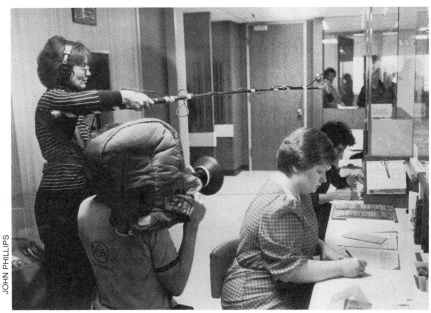

The making of Laura Sky's Yes We Can

5

STEPHANIE URDANG

solidarity for a local or international social movement. It could be that they are using a film showing for fundraising, or simply for entertainment. Often a film showing is a combination of all these goals.

As women who work with DEC Films, a distributor of Canadian and international social issue films and videos, we have found that all of this activity and growth has not only opened up new possibilities for women's culture, but also created new needs. Many of the films and videos in the DEC Films collection are about women, by women, and for women. These films form one focus of our work as a whole, and inform our perspective. We think it is important to build audiences — and especially new and larger audiences — for the films.

As film distributors we also provide a link between producers and users. We try to acquire films for distribution based on community needs and requests. In turn we pay back 50 per cent of the income received from sales and rentals to the producer.

Because our day-to-day work brings us into regular contact with film users, we often get asked for help in finding the right film or video for a particular audience. We get requests for information on the details of organizing small and large showings, or for programming and planning film festivals or film series. This book has been written partly in response to these requests. It forms as well an attempt to provide practical information for people who are using film as a tool for education and for expanding and mobilizing audiences.

We also want to encourage wide-ranging critical analysis of what is being seen, and to suggest ways of building successful post-showing discussion. Again, this comes out of our experience in working collectively with DEC Films to select films for distribution, assessing their potential use and thinking about how they work. The section "Taking a Closer Look at Feminist Filmmaking" is our attempt to offer some approaches for evaluating and discussing the women's films we see. We hope, in general, that the book will help build confidence for both showing and discussing film and video in all their forms and variables.

Images in Action is also aimed at those who want to encourage an independent film movement, one separate from the product of Hollywood and the mass market. It is difficult to escape that Hollywood

NFB

From 'Would I Ever Like To Work'

product, whether at the local theatre or at home on the TV set. This makes it all the more important, we believe, to develop an audience for independent film. These independent films are often less well known and on the surface perhaps not as glossy or enticing as Hollywood films, not as easy to take. But they are, we would argue, much more valuable. Besides reflecting and discussing and coming out of our own experiences and concerns, they carry a sense of intensity and excitement that is most often missing in standard fare.

Very few independent feature fiction films — much less documentary films — get theatrical release. The few that do are usually shown only in the large urban areas. Part of our aim is to help make independent films more available, and to help provide others with the information necessary to make them more widely available, especially on a local, community level. Our distribution work has been built partly around this premise, of attempting to get the work of independent filmmakers, including women filmmakers, known and shown, understood and appreciated.

By offering practical information and advice on finding films, and on programming and planning small and large group showings, we try to demystify, but not simplify, the use of film and video. Our main hope is that this book will prove to be a useful tool for all users of films, whether women or men. We hope it will encourage the use of films and videos as resources for critical use and active challenge. We especially want the book to be a celebration of women's achievement in film: to validate the important work that is being done and to help enlarge the audience and appreciation for that work.

HELENA SOLBERG-LADD

Throughout this book, unless otherwise indicated, the term "film" refers to films, videos, and slide-tape shows. We are not, however, suggesting that these forms are the same, either in production or use. While we want to promote all of them, each has advantages and disadvantages. The kind of equipment you have access to partly determines the medium you choose to use, as do questions of cost, artistic form, and content. Together, films, videos, and slide-tape shows by women form a major part of a growing and changing women's culture.

Media formats and terms used in this guide

Film

Although it is more expensive to produce than video or slideshows, 16mm film is the most common film format used by organizers, educators, and community groups. A 16mm film projects easily on a large screen, providing sharp and clear images, which along with good sound can carry a great dramatic and emotional impact. Projectors for 16mm film can be rented or borrowed fairly easily. They can be temperamental, especially if they are old and over-used, but they operate on simple principles and are usually not hard to operate.

An alternative to 16mm film is 8mm or Super-8, most commonly used for home movies and experimental filmmaking. Super-8 or 8mm projectors are smaller and not interchangeable with 16mm projectors, although they operate in much the same way.

Movie theatres usually show 35 mm films, a more expensive format that requires trained, licensed projectionists. The equipment is generally only available in movie theatres — it is not as portable as 16mm or Super-8. Often, however, films shown in theatres are available on 16mm, and increasingly on video as well.

Video

Video as a medium has the advantage of light and easily portable production equipment, and the tape is less expensive to buy and process. Because video cameras are smaller than 16mm cameras, video production also has the advantage of being less intrusive than film, and is often better able to capture a sense of intimacy or group process.

The mechanics of video showings are also more flexible than film. The tape can be stopped in an instant, easily rewound, and played again starting from whatever precise spot is wanted; this makes it an extremely useful tool for small group discussion. A room does not need to be dark to show videos, so the atmosphere can be relaxed and informal, encouraging people to participate in discussion both during and after the showing. Video machines can play information continuously during conferences and at display tables — attracting attention and offering people a non-threatening atmosphere for viewing and learning. As well, video-tape is less expensive to rent than 16mm film, and more and more people have VCRs at home.

There are two parts to video-viewing equipment: a video-cassette recorder (VCR) and a monitor (often a TV set). A complication is that there are three different kinds of video systems (¾" cassette, ½" Beta cassette, and ½" VHS cassette) and they are not interchangeable. So make sure the various parts of the system you rent or borrow are compatible. And beware that videos made in Europe, Australia, and Asia are the PAL or SECAM systems, and are not compatible with NTSC, the North American system.

The texture of video images is different from film images. The picture is not as sharp. Video images can feel more immediate and personal, whereas film images, because of their larger size and greater clarity, tend to carry a more intense emotional impact and take on a "larger than life" quality.

Anyone who likes to take pictures and has access to a tape recorder can make a slide-tape show. When the images are strong and the slides and soundtrack are arranged to create a sense of fluid movement, slide-tape shows can have a solid impact. They can also be stopped at any point, and are easily divided into parts. When the format and equipment are simple (for example, a 140-slide carousel and one audio cassette), slide-tape shows are easy to use, and the equipment is much cheaper to rent or purchase than films and videos. For this reason, slide-tape shows are useful for chronically underfunded women's groups.

A note on independent filmmaking

Many feminist films are independent productions. An independent film or video is "created by persons who are not regularly employed by any corporation, network, institution or agency which determines either the form or content of the materials which he or she produces."*

---

* This definition is used by the Association of Independent Video and Filmmakers (AIVF) in its *Recommendations for the Future of Public Broadcasting*, Jan. 25, 1978.

Many independent productions do not find commercial or institutional support. So, while independent producers often have artistic control over their productions, they also have to work extremely hard, with little or no pay, to keep their productions afloat and to stay independent of imposed criteria for form or content. Women face the added difficulty of having less than equal opportunity for technical training and financial backing.

It is especially important, then, that independent women filmmakers get the support of the communities — especially the women — who use the product of their labours. Some of that support comes directly from film use: A large percentage of the rental fee of an independently produced film goes back to the filmmaker.

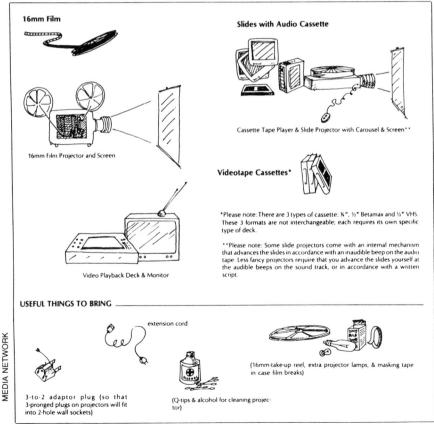

16mm Film

16mm Film Projector and Screen

Video Playback Deck & Monitor

Slides with Audio Cassette

Cassette Tape Player & Slide Projector with Carousel & Screen**

Videotape Cassettes*

*Please note: There are 3 types of cassette: ¾", ½" Betamax and ½" VHS. These 3 formats are not interchangeable; each requires its own specific type of deck.

**Please note: Some slide projectors come with an internal mechanism that advances the slides in accordance with an inaudible beep on the audio tape. Less fancy projectors require that you advance the slides yourself at the audible beeps on the sound track, or in accordance with a written script.

USEFUL THINGS TO BRING

extension cord

3-to-2 adaptor plug (so that 3-pronged plugs on projectors will fit into 2-hole wall sockets)

(Q-tips & alcohol for cleaning projector)

(16mm take-up reel, extra projector lamps, & masking tape in case film breaks)

Designing Film Programs

A speaker tends to relate to people on an intellectual level, while a film can open you up and make you receptive to a broad range of experiences. A film touches the heart and mind at the same time.

Three women were discussing an upcoming meeting on women in developing countries for their Development and Peace group. Ann said, "Obviously, we have to have a film on poverty." "No," said Barb, "we need a film that shows culture, dignity, humour — in other words, people as human beings." "I don't agree with either of you," said Susan. "We need a film on politics."*

In order to find the right film, video, or slide-tape show for any kind of showing, you have to think first of all about what you want it to say to the particular audience. You need to have a clear idea of your aims for the discussion and consider the expectations and knowledge level of the audience.

There can be a great many reasons why you and your group or organization want to show films:

- Provide information
- Encourage group discussion
- Examine the complexities of issues
- Reach a policy or stand concerning an issue
- Move people into action
- Provide support for the goals of a group or organization
- Offer support to other groups and people
- Entertain
- Educate
- Attract new membership to a group

The list could certainly go on and on. While no one film will likely meet all your needs — or the needs of an audience or an educational process — a film showing can be an excellent way to attract and stimulate a group of people, and it can lead to a discussion that covers many aspects of the issue or issues you want to deal with.

Some initial thoughts on programming

Film programming means selecting films and organizing showings for a particular purpose. It involves deciding whether to run a single event or a series, as well as getting films and deciding when, where, and how to show them. Whether you are planning a film program for a special International Women's Day celebration, a weekend union conference, a peace day, a cultural festival, a noon-hour series in a workplace, or a school course: An extravaganza of women's films is likely not only to elicit thought-provoking responses, but also to be fun.

One of the first things to remember is that no programmer is

---

* Adapted from Neil Taylor and Robin Richardson, *Seeing and Perceiving: Films in a World of Change* (Suffolk, England: Concord Film Council, 1979).

neutral. Although you can choose films that explore an issue from more than one point of view, personal and political biases will inevitably influence your choices. There will be certain things that you — as an individual or a group — will want to do with a showing, certain goals you want to reach. As a programmer, you are not obliged to present all sides of any issue. It is quite acceptable to program from a particular point of view. Programmers can be as expansive or focused as they wish.

A programmer can select unusual combinations of films to encourage critical thought. Your group or committee might want to lobby another group to support a cause that on first glance is not related to that group's work. Although it is not always appropriate to plan confrontation, sometimes it helps to take risks. For instance, showing a film on Salvadorean women in combat at a forum on racism and sexism, or taking a film on lesbian issues to a union or church meeting considering human rights, can be thought-provoking and stimulating.

Creativity in programming comes when you decide *why* to show particular films, and *how* the films will work as part of an agenda: whether they are interspersed with speakers, cultural events, or meetings, or whether they stand on their own. When you are organizing a series or festival, the *order of events* is often key to engaging an audience. If you begin with films that are likely to draw an audience — award-winners, films that focus on topical social issues, dramatic or entertaining productions — this can build up interest in the issue. It makes the audience more receptive to other more off-beat or seemingly obscure films.

The terms *series* and *festival* are often used interchangeably. But a film series is a number of associated film showings scheduled at regular times, usually over a lengthy period of time. A film festival is a program scheduled for a short period of time, sometimes with several films showing simultaneously in different locations. Both series and festivals can highlight or celebrate particular films or issues.

Whether series or festivals, public film showings mean it is difficult to predict the makeup of an audience, and even harder to know what the audience response will be. Often people will have the time or inclination to see only a small number of films in an extensive program. Nevertheless, it is important to plan an integrated and carefully considered selection, examining the message, quality, and emotional impact of each film.

From Women in Arms

15

Suggestions for Designing a Film Program:

- Move from films with general information to films exploring issues in a specific, in-depth way.
- Begin with films that supply factual information and then show some that raise questions and analyse.
- Move from historical to contemporary-issue films if the historical material has a special or particularly engaging meaning to the audience.
- Or move from newer films to older ones; current films carry a fresh immediacy and help develop the context for older resources on subjects that are perhaps less familiar or that at first glance might seem of less interest.
- When you are showing more than one film at a time, in different locations, try not to schedule, in the same time slot, films that cover similar issues.
- Try to balance the rhythms and energy levels of the different films; for example, decide which ones will leave people feeling energetic and ready for action, and which ones will leave people feeling reflective or overwhelmed.
- Vary the running times; this will help to retain the audience's interest; for instance, a short animated film shown along with a feature-length documentary can be more effective than two medium-length documentaries on the same subject.
- Vary the styles and genres of the films you plan to show — for example, documentary, fiction, animation, and experimental — within the same program.

Building a program: Eight ideas

Following are some concrete ideas about how to program films. Some of the ideas refer to specific films, while others consider different types of films or films on specific issues. Although we present them as a list, none of the ideas are meant to be exclusive of one another; they can overlap. We hope that you will be able to add to or adapt the ideas in this list to your particular needs.

1. One Issue from Different Perspectives

Purpose of the program: to get at the complexities of an issue

to minimize and debunk stereotyping of situations or people

Example One: Show two films on women in non-traditional work. The first film contains factual information that analyses the jobs available to women in Canada. It shows how most women who work outside the home perform traditional women's jobs and earn lower pay than men. The film documents both the gains women have made in jobs traditionally reserved for men, and the need for widespread affirmative action programs. The second film features interviews with several women already working in non-traditional jobs, and shows both the satisfactions and difficulties in their work. Both films are documentary, but the first relies on statistical information and analysis, while the second film presents the subjects as experts, and relies on their testimonies for its analysis.

Example Two: Show two films on abortion. One focuses on women's right to choose and have control over reproduction, while the other concentrates on the personal dilemmas of women who choose to have an abortion.

2. One Issue Using Different Film Styles

Purpose of the program: to promote use of a wide variety of women's films

to show that the way a film is made affects the viewer's understanding of the issues

Example: Show and compare two films on violence against women, *We Will Not Be Beaten* and *Behind Closed Doors.* The documentary *We Will Not Be Beaten* uses extensive interviews in which women talk about their experiences of abuse. *Behind Closed Doors,* a short experimental film, shows no women on the screen. Instead, the camera closely watches a bedroom disintegrate from meticulous cleanliness to complete disarray; on the soundtrack a collage of women's voices graphically describes their personal experiences.

3. One Issue From Opposing Viewpoints

Purpose of the program: to provoke an audience response, rather than to put forward a balanced point of view

Example One: Show an early Hollywood film that uses blatant stereotypes of woman as sex goddess and faithful wife, together with a contemporary women's film that presents complex characters.

Example Two: Show an explicitly sexist film along with *Killing Us Softly*, a film that exposes and analyses sex role stereotyping in advertising and in mainstream media images of women.

4. Bringing the Issues Home: Films from Other Countries

Purpose of the program: to develop tolerance and understanding of cultural differences

to encourage international solidarity among women

to make concrete connections between women with differing nationalities, histories, and priorities

Example One: Show *Selbe — One Among Many*, a film depicting the daily life of a rural woman in Senegal, together with a Canadian film on women's work. Both of these films focus on the undervaluing of women's work and the reality of women's capabilities.

Example Two: Show *La Operación*, a film on forced sterilization of women in Puerto Rico, along with a Canadian film on birth control. These films point out the different meanings of "choice" for Third World women, and immigrant, Native, and non-Native Canadians.

Example Three: Show two films on Third World women from different countries to bring out similarities and differences between women's lives in those countries and possible parallels with women in Canada.

5. About Then and Now

Purpose of the program: to validate women's place in history, which has often been hidden

to compare the past with the present

Example: Show Iolande Cadrin-Rossignol's dramatization of the life of Laure Gaudreault, the organizer of the first women teachers' union in Quebec, along with Lee Grant's film *The Willmar Eight*, about bank workers who went on strike for over a year in an attempt to organize the first bank union in Minnesota. These films can be used to point out the parallels between social conditions in Quebec in the 1930s and the mid-western United States in the late 1970s.

STEPHANIE URDANG

From Selbe

From Willmar Eight *by Lee Grant*

6. From the Same Director

Purpose of the program: to support women's culture and celebrate achievements

to look at the growth, changes, and style of one producer

to give the filmmakers and audience a chance to meet each other

Example One: Highlight films by a documentary filmmaker and invite her to speak about her work and its connection with the women's movement.

Example Two: Highlight a video producer who uses a unique and innovative style to address women's concerns. The producer can tell how and where a resource was produced and she can bring the video, its attitudes, and the process of making it closer to the audience.

7. Linking Issues

Purpose of the program: to widen community support for different issues

to link issues for the audience

Example One: Show *The Clean Sweep (La Grande Remue-Menage)*, which explores the roots of sexism in Quebec society, along with a Quebec video, *You Might Think You're Superior, But I Think I'm Equal*, which looks at how socialization in the school system reinforces discrimination against people of colour. These films can be used to draw links between the issues of sexism and racism.

Example Two: Show films that are not explicitly on women's issues, but deal with related social issues such as the environment or disarmament, to help analyse power structures and develop strategies for action on these issues. Resources such as *In Our Water*, a film about the pollution of a rural community's water supply by a toxic waste dump and a local resident's campaign to change the situation, or *Stronger Than Before*, a video-tape on women in the peace movement in Canada, raise interesting questions regarding women's strategy in challenging male-dominated power structures.

8. Resources That Depict Regional Differences and Similarities

Purpose of the program: to draw out similarities and differences between women

to inform about issues involving women living in other areas

Example: Show a film about Newfoundland women in the fishing industry along with a film on women in the textile industry in Toronto. These films contrast different working conditions and living environments and contribute to an enlarged understanding of different regions.

Organizing Small-Group Screenings

Once you've decided that you want to show a film or films to a group of people, and have developed certain ideas about the purpose and type of program, it's time to start thinking about organizing the event itself. In this chapter we look at the various tasks involved in showing a film to a small group — which we define as an audience of anywhere from a handful of people to fifty or so.

Carrying off a successful screening for a small group of people can be relatively straightforward if you pay careful attention to a small list of details. The planning runs from choosing a film and a time and location for the showing, to making sure you have extra bulbs available for a projector, to seeing that there is wheelchair access or child care if necessary. For all of the details and decisions there are basic guidelines to help see you safely through the process and make sure the showing comes off as smoothly as possible. And along the way there are also various embellishments; although they aren't crucial, they can add to the education, entertainment, and fundraising possibilities of the showing.

We've broken the tasks into four parts. First comes an initial planning stage: previewing the film and considering the audience you want to see it. Second comes the matter of organizing the many details of the event. A third task involves planning the specifics of leading a discussion. And a fourth, very important task — often forgotten — is to plan for an evaluation of the event.

We especially want to emphasize the importance of planning for a discussion after a film showing. A discussion allows people in the audience to hear what others think about the film, to express their own opinions, and otherwise exchange ideas and debate different points of view. Sometimes it's a chance to get information about the film from the filmmakers themselves or others with special knowledge. Showing a film without a discussion can leave people feeling confused or let down — feeling that something important is slipping by. Others may feel excited and full of new energy and concern. They may want a chance to channel their emotions and ideas and think about action, and a discussion can help them do this.

One further note about this chapter: Although it is aimed at small-group screenings, we hope the information can also be used for designing film programs for series, festivals, or large public screenings.

Previewing: What to look for

Always try to preview a film, to look at it before confirming your order, or at least before showing it to an audience. Previewing builds a discussion leader's confidence, and helps ensure that the event will go as smoothly as possible and help accomplish your purpose. Previewing can also help you anticipate possible problems. It tells you exactly what is in the film. It tells you the filmmaker's approach to the issue and lets you assess whether her biases are compatible with your own — or perhaps whether her approach will create the kind of contrast or controversy you are looking for.

You'll be able to prepare questions about the film in order to move the discussion along, to deal with difficult questions, or to deal with the silence that is as natural in an audience as it is terrifying to a discussion leader.

Not all film distributors are able to let you preview films before you rent them. If it is not possible to preview, request a synopsis, reviews, and any other available written material from the distributor. Set aside time to preview the film as early as possible after it arrives for the showing. Even a cursory look just before the showing, preferably with other people, will help you prepare for the discussion, and is definitely better than no preview at all.

It is useful to keep in mind that filmmakers convey their messages through their technical, artistic, political, and personal choices. No film, whether documentary or fiction, is objective. A preview provides a chance to think about the basic elements of a film, and to try to discern and analyse not only what a film says, but also what it *says it says* — which is sometimes quite different.

When previewing, then, you should look not only at the content but also at the style of the film. Doing this helps to clarify both your own point of view and the film's.

Basic Elements of a Film:

- Sound: narration, music, interview, sound effects, background noise, dialogue, voice-over.
- Visuals: camera movement, varying camera angles (from above, below, at same level as subject), camera distance from subject (close-up, long shot), use of photographs, animation, graphics, printed words, use of film stock (colour or black and white, grainy or sharp texture), use of lighting (light/dark).
- Editing: mixing the sound together with the visuals (synchronized or non-synchronized), arranging the images (chronological order, disjunctive, following a story-line or linear order, using excerpts from television and other films).

Questions to Ask Yourself When Previewing

1. Does the film have a clear point of view? What is that point of view?
2. Does the film take a stand on the questions it raises? What is its stand?

3. Does the film's point of view reinforce, oppose, or overlook your own?
4. Does the soundtrack support the visuals, or does it give a different message?
5. Does the film deal adequately with the issue or issues? Is anything missing or dealt with inadequately?
6. Do you need to give the audience background information before the film showing, or would that prejudice their response to the film?

An Example Preview: The Film "A Wives' Tale"

A Wives' Tale is a seventy-three minute 16mm colour film, produced and directed in 1980 by Sophie Bissonette, Joyce Rock, and Martin Duckworth.

The lives of the 160,000 residents of Sudbury are determined by the rhythm of the world nickel market and primarily by one company, Inco. In 1978, miners went out on a strike that was to become one of the most important battles in Canadian labour history.

But this film is not about the strikers; it is about the "Wives Supporting the Strike," the women who organized to support the miners and their families. The filmmakers lived for four and a half months with the strikers in their homes, and during that time captured both the private and public moments of their lives.

A Wives' Tale is a dramatic documentary using an observational style. The filmmakers document meetings in small kitchens and large union halls. They use historical photographs mixed with a narrative account of a woman's life in Sudbury to link the past with the present. Yet there is actually little narration in the film. For the most part people speak for themselves.

Questions for Discussion

Note: Before delving into questions of style and content during a discussion period after a film showing, it is important to give the audience time to express their first impressions and emotions.

Style:
1. What sequence did you find most powerful? Why?
2. Was the camera sensitive to the people being filmed, or did it invade their privacy?
3. Did you notice the music in the film? Did it affect your response?

A poster from the film **A** Wives Tale *by Sophie Bissonnette, Martin Duckworth, and Joyce Rock*

4. Were the women in the film allowed to speak for themselves?

Emotion/Content:
1. How did the personal stories in the historical section affect you?
2. Did you know Sudbury has a large French-speaking population?
3. Do you think the film is for or against unions?
4. Do you think the union is for or against women?

During the discussion after a film, organizers rely on the audience to offer their individual reactions to what they saw on the screen and to talk about how those reactions agree or conflict with those of other viewers.

A responsive audience and a lively discussion are a clear indication of success. This kind of success requires that organizers and

Considering your audience

discussion leaders understand the background, expectations, and relationship of the audience to themselves.

Your Relationship to the Audience

1. Are you a member of the group you are showing the film to? If so, ask the group for input on selection of the film and the sequence of events at the showing.
2. If you are not a member of the group, but have simply been engaged to work at organizing the event or leading the discussion: Meet in advance with the group, or its representatives, to determine their goals and expectations for the event. It is important at the same time that you are straightforward about your own goals and expectations.
3. What do you want from the audience?
4. What does the audience want from you?
5. Is there likely to be the opportunity or need for follow-up action after the event?
6. Will the film be fitting into an event that has already been planned, or do you have input into the planning process?
7. Do members of the audience know each other? If not, introductions (if it's a small enough audience) can help people feel more comfortable about speaking out.
8. Does the audience have a common interest or understanding? Is its position clear?
9. Will everyone understand the film? What extra information can you provide to help clarify it?

When you do not know the answers to the last three questions, the discussion can begin with some general questions about the issues being addressed in the film. Ask for a show of hands for questions such as: "How many of you know someone who has been sexually harassed?" "Do any of you know someone who has lost a job just because she was a woman?" "How many know a woman who has been raped?" The show of hands will help the leader assess the group's experience without asking people to acknowledge any direct personal experience they might feel uncomfortable disclosing.

If you find that people are not familiar with the issues presented in the film, a general introduction sheet on terms and assumptions made in the film can help fill the gaps.

Different Audiences, Different Approaches

1. **All Women:** Women's films often touch on personal concerns and stimulate women to talk about their own experiences. When the audience has a common goal and there is a safe environment in which to speak out, there is greater potential for expressing feelings, frustrations, and anger, and a common urge to fight back. The result can frequently be a fertile ground for women to organize to change their situations. (As might be expected, this interaction can happen a little more easily when the women involved in the discussion already know each other.)

   At the same time, women's experiences — and their reactions to a film — are quite diverse. Some women may be threatened by the testimony of a lesbian in a film or discussion. A Native woman may feel that a discussion among white women has little to do with her own life. A discussion facilitator will be better able to challenge stereotypes and bridge divisions if for her part she is aware of and able to deal constructively with issues of homophobia or racism.

2. **Women and Men:** Topics such as battering, rape, pornography, or sexual harassment provoke strong emotional responses from everyone, and there can be obstacles to discussing these issues openly in a mixed group of women and men. When a film raises these issues from a woman's point of view, the presence of men can silence or inhibit the women, regardless of the men's personal points of view. One way to avoid this problem is to have separate men's and women's discussion groups. A discussion leader can point out that this is useful for both sexes, because in both cases it helps allow for more open discussion and participation. It is still possible to have a joint discussion after the separate ones have finished.

3. **Different Languages:** If the language of the film is not the first language of the group, your selection considerations should include:

   - A film that doesn't rely heavily on a language soundtrack to get its message across. This could include a fiction film with lots of action and straightforward plot, or a lyrical film that mainly uses visuals to get its point across.
   - A film that uses dialogue between characters rather than narration or voice-over, because when you see people speaking it is easier to understand.

27

- A film with appropriate subtitles when there are two major language groups in the audience.

4. **Different Races:** Many new films are beginning to acknowledge the experiences and histories of women of colour, especially as more of them begin to produce their own films. This development is worth pointing out, especially to audiences unaware of those experiences. Unfortunately, many films still do not acknowledge women of colour. In those cases, raising the problem of invisibility can challenge audiences and help them look at other films with a newly critical eye.

5. **Different Cultural Backgrounds:** Cultural traditions contribute to a variety of different perceptions of society. For discussions in a multicultural group it helps to acknowledge openly these different cultural perceptions and to make sure the group deals with them, and especially that the group works to avoid stereotyped responses.

6. **Different Classes:** When you are selecting a resource, ask yourself in whose interest it was produced, and think about whether the filmmaker considered the concept of class. For the most part working-class women are under-represented in films. Middle-class women's experiences are often portrayed as all women's experiences. Yet women experience the same problems in different ways according to their class. For example, the economic threat that is an aspect of sexual harassment may not be as great for a professional woman as for an office or factory worker.

7. **Regional, Rural, Urban Differences:** A rural group may find it difficult to identify with a film set in an urban community. At the same time, interesting parallels can emerge when, for example, farm women discuss a film on occupational hazards for women in factories: Farm women also experience hazards on the job. In Canada, regional differences are as great as rural and urban differences, and a discussion facilitator needs to take them into account.

8. **Variations in Ability:** Be sure to consider the wheelchair accessibility of the film showing wherever and whenever possible. If those attending have hearing difficulties it might help to show a film that is visually powerful and has subtitles, or provide a corner with a signer and a focused light. For a video showing a signer can be positioned next to one of the monitors.

We showed a film but the take-up reel was too small. It took ages of careful hand rewinding to disentangle almost a mile of celluloid.

We weren't able to visit the space ahead of time. It turned out that the room had a fridge in it that was incredibly noisy, and we couldn't figure out how to turn it off — so the film was very hard to hear.

One of the blinds wouldn't come down so we thought the room couldn't be blacked out. But someone came up with the idea of tying a few coats together and hanging them over the windows.

Everything was perfectly organized, and then . . . a three-pronged plug in a two-pronged socket — the ultimate disaster.

The projector cord couldn't reach the socket. We'd forgotten to bring an extension cord.

Not all disasters can be avoided, but you can eliminate many of them if you give yourself plenty of lead-time. Although not always necessary, it is reasonable to begin planning the details of the event some six weeks before your showing. Among other things, you have to book the film properly, arrange for a place to show the film, organize a budget, take care of the necessary equipment, and prepare for the discussion. Above all, you have to let the intended audience know that the showing is happening.

Booking the Film

To reserve a film it is best to contact the distributor as far in advance as possible. You can either telephone or write, depending on the time available. The information you need to give to the distributor includes:

1. The date of the showing (and an alternative date if possible).
2. The name and address of the person or group.
3. The shipping instructions — you and the distributor need to agree upon the exact shipping method (air, bus, mail, courier service), the place of delivery and pick-up, and the means of paying the shipping costs.
4. Confirmation of how the film will be returned, and when (usually the distributor wants it back the day after the showing).
5. Your contact person and phone number in case a problem arises with your film booking.

Information you should get from the distributor:

1. The format (8mm or 16mm, ¾" or ½" Beta or VHS video), as well as the running time and language; for example, whether there are subtitles. (For more information on formats, see "Media Formats and Terms Used in This Guide.")
2. The cost.
3. The equipment necessary to show the film.
4. Written information on the film and filmmaker.
5. The possibility of previewing the film.
6. Written confirmation of your booking.
7. The technical quality of the film.

Arranging a Room

Booking a film and booking a space to show it in have to be done hand in hand. Both have to be done early on. The space you use needs to be suitable for both a film showing (it can be darkened) and a discussion (comfortable seating where people can see and hear each other well). Make sure that you have everything you need: a screen, white wall, or sheet (preferably with no wrinkles); tables and chairs; electrical outlets, extension cords, and three-pronged adaptors; curtains or shades to darken the room. If you haven't used the room before, someone should check it out in advance. You never know what unforeseen obstacles might greet you.

Informing the Audience

Whether you do it through a newsletter, an announcement or ad, a special mailing, or a phone tree, it is crucial to inform audiences about the details of the event. Include the name and subject of the film, the exact date, time, and location of the showing, the names of any resource people, and information on special plans for the event. You should let people know if you are having a well known speaker or if the film has won awards.

Costs

The budget for a showing can include:

1. Cost of film rental and shipping.
2. Cost of the room for showing.

3. Cost of paper and mailing for publicizing the event.
4. Rental cost for projection equipment.
5. Cost of refreshments.

Note: If the organizing group has no money, and you're not charging for admission, you can usually offset your costs by passing the hat or asking for a donation at the event.

Equipment

Arrange in advance for any equipment you need: a 16mm film projector, a slide projector and tape recorder, or a video-cassette recorder and monitor (TV set). Make sure that the monitor and playback units are compatible with the cable adaptors. If you have a colour video you should have a colour television set.

Public libraries sometimes lend projectors. School boards, churches, and unions often have 16mm and video equipment. Projectors will sometimes eat films, so try to have an experienced projectionist on hand to operate the machinery. It also helps to have scotch tape available to repair the film in case it rips.

It is not hard to learn how to use a projector, so if you are going to show films frequently, get a projectionist to show you how, and take the opportunity to practise until you feel secure (it won't take long).

The Day Before

Arrange to pick up the necessary equipment — the film, projector, screen, appropriate-sized take-up reel, extension cords, three-pronged to two-pronged adaptor, any additional tables and chairs, and if possible extra sound and light bulbs for the projector.

The Day of the Event: Setting Up

Some basic guidelines:

1. Be there an hour before your group arrives.
2. Set up the equipment, test it for sound, picture, light, and focus.
3. Make sure the projected image will clear everyone's head and that everyone can see (for example, make sure that pillars or poles do not obstruct any views).

31

4. Locate and identify light switches.
5. Tape down extension cords with masking tape or scotch tape so no one trips over them or pulls them from the outlet accidentally.
6. Arrange the seating to suit the needs of the particular audience.
7. Prepare and set out refreshments, if any.

Leading the discussion

• Experiences • Situations • Challenges • Problems • Solutions

Linking Issues

"I used a film on women's participation in the Nicaraguan revolution with women's peace organizations. The orientation of most women in the group was towards non-violent strategies. I wanted to open this up for debate by giving the group an opportunity to understand experiences of women from another country. The film challenged the group and there was a long, interesting discussion."

Speaking Out

"The day I saw a film on domestic violence at the transition house was the first time I had talked to anyone about the pain my children and I had gone through."

Taking Action

"After screening a film on the wives of striking miners organizing in Sudbury, a group of women saw how they could start up a committee here in Cape Breton to support their union and husbands in a coal strike. And they did."

Relating Personal Experiences

"Working in the trade union movement changed the way I look at films. Usually I use films related to my workplace, and until there's a certain level of organization, I use films that I think are not controversial. But they often turn out to be controversial in their own way. They allow women to talk about their own experience, and that really works in a deep way."

From Women in Arms *by Victoria Schultz*

Dialogue Among the Audience

"We showed a film on women and unions to give women an opportunity to talk about their own experience. The men in the group wanted to talk about their perceptions of women and unions. As the discussion leader, I was considering whether to redirect the conversation by posing another question or by intervening directly. Then a woman in the audience spoke up. She said she was pleased that the men were interested but she felt the discussion was beginning to parallel the problem in the union movement — where women aren't normally given space to present their own concerns."

Cultural Challenges

"I was invited to a film showing for Greek women on violence against women. Most of the women were older than me, and were proud housekeepers with a strong commitment to the nuclear family. The film had two problems. First the woman in the film had a messy house, and most of these Greek women felt that was a disgrace. Secondly, the tragedy of breaking up the family is as great for them as the situation of a battered woman. But the discussion afterwards challenged some ideas — such as the notion that 'women are to blame' — and created a good consciousness-raising session. The Greek translation was excellent and that was important."

"Preaching to the Converted"

"A group of women from different organizations were screening a film on women's music and the power of emotion and social awareness behind women's creativity. Most of the audience was responding positively, when one woman said, 'We're just preaching to the converted here.' It was a definite put-down. I had learned a lot from the film, and felt that the discussion was helping women from different groups discover shared assumptions. It's one thing to take up the challenge of involving other people in the women's movement, but that was not our main purpose. The comment stifled further discussion."

Some Suggestions for Leading a Discussion

From Quel Numero, What Number?

You don't have to be an expert on film or on the subject of the film you show in order to be an effective leader. You do need enthusiasm and commitment. The more thoroughly you are able to plan, the more at ease you will be. Careful planning and thought can turn a film showing into a dynamic community event.

Remember that not all groups have the same potential. If the discussion does not meet your expectations, it may have as much or more to do with the audience than it does with you. You are not solely responsible for the success of the discussion, and it helps to be flexible in your expectations, ready to respond to the interests and potential of the audience.

Also, if you are not personally comfortable or at ease working with a sizable group of people, don't forget that a discussion does not have to be led by just one person. Two leaders can support one another and help field questions or channel them back to the audience.

Not all of the following practical suggestions for planning and leading a discussion will apply to your circumstances. Feel free to change the ingredients and adapt the recipe to your audience and personal tastes. And remember: In any discussion it is perfectly okay to come right out and say, "I don't know."

The central task is to help people talk to each other about what they have just seen and to look at the issues critically.

1. **Know your audience:** the make-up of the group, approximate size. See the section *"Considering Your Audience"* earlier in this chapter for further information.

2. **Know the format of the event:** What is the sequence of events? Who will introduce the film? Will there be special guests? Will you divide into small groups afterwards for discussion?

3. **Make your audience feel comfortable:** A welcoming atmosphere and seating arrangement where everyone can see each other (for example, in a circle rather than rows) make people feel relaxed and invited to participate. It helps to have people introduce themselves if the group is small enough.

4. **Introduce the film:** Be brief, give general information about the evening's events, about the filmmaker, the date of the film, name of the country of origin, and the running time. It can be a mistake to warn an audience about their possible responses, or to summarize the film — let it speak for itself, and let the audience react on their own terms. There are no right or wrong ways to respond.

5. **Begin the discussion:** After showing the film, give the audience a few minutes to be silent, stretch, and let their feelings settle. Don't panic during this time. Discussions usually take a few minutes to get under way. If the film made an impact a discussion will happen, and it is crucial to allow emotional responses to come out before delving into analysis. Questions like "How do you feel about what you have seen?" or "What are your initial impressions?" are good ways to start. (There's more on this in "Question Raising," later in this chapter.)

6. **Emotional responses:** During the showing itself you might note down the times when people clap, cry, fidget, or laugh, and talk about these moments as a means of starting a discussion about emotional responses to the film. Part of the job, too, is to remind people that emotional responses to a film will always differ, and that the range of responses can cover a whole spectrum of feeling. And that it is important to explore this full spectrum in order to

A job description for discussion leaders

35

understand the relationship between filmmaker, issue/subject, and audience.

7. **Focus on the film:** In order to maximize learning from the film, it is important not to move too quickly from discussing and evaluating the film to forming strategy for community action. One way to focus is to ask the audience about specific sequences in the film, or to try and get at the parts that most impressed people. Have questions prepared in advance, if possible.

8. **Clarify and link individual concerns:** If it seems the group does not completely understand a question or an answer — or if you are not sure yourself — it is helpful to try to rephrase the point. It is also useful to draw connections between the different comments being made. As well it is important to recognize and respect differences of opinion so that personal conflicts don't take hold. In order to put the conflict into perspective a discussion leader can reiterate what she sees as the major points.

9. **Keep the discussion on track:** If members of the audience roam onto a tangent, it is all right to interject, politely and firmly. But be sensitive to important tangents.

10. **Summarize when necessary:** A flip chart or large sheets of paper on the wall can help focus the discussion by recording issues, controversies and decisions.

11. **Direct discussion based on audience needs:** This can range from asking questions that will lead to a greater understanding of the issues raised to helping the group brainstorm strategies for possible actions.

12. **Help find ways to follow up:** If follow-up activities or actions are part of the group's goals, the discussion leader should keep this in mind. When the discussion/evaluation of the film itself seems complete or exhausted, channel the discussion in the direction of possible action. If necessary, choose one theme to follow through on. Ask the group to write down their concerns and then list them in order of priority. This part of the discussion period is particularly important when an audience is emotionally moved or confused about the discussion and wants to continue.

13. **Wrapping up: Be brief.** Summarize major points and any follow-up tasks people agreed to take on. Thank everyone for coming.

14. **Distribute and collect evaluations:** It is important to evaluate both the film and your role as discussion leader. (See section on evaluation later in this chapter.)

A whole range of activities and ideas can be adapted for use in a wide variety of situations. They can encourage discussion and involve the audience in the issues, but it should be noted that they are not equally useful for all films or all audiences.

    The top priorities are to be sensitive to the group's needs and keep the discussion open to all the opinions that arise. As discussion leader you do not have to deny or hide your opinion. Also, not everyone will want to participate; you should respect the right of women who do not want to speak out.

Ideas and techniques for creating discussion*

Question Raising: From Awareness to Action

"Question raising" is a method of popular education used in group situations to locate and discuss both personal and social problems. It is also a useful way to help groups using a film to analyse a situation and find solutions. It involves using a list of questions to help a group get started. List them on a flip chart but don't feel you must go through all of them. If possible, record responses as well on a flip chart. They may come in handy at a later date.

    If the size of the group is too large for everyone to participate, you can divide into smaller groups, allotting time at the end to bring everyone back together to report on and evaluate their discussions.

1. **Description:** What did you see, hear, or feel about the film? What do you think is happening? How do you feel about it?

2. **Personal Association:** Have you or anyone you know experienced anything you saw in the film? Do you identify with any person in the film or any problems expressed?

3. **Social Relationship:** How is your experience similar to the experience of others in the audience? How is it different? Do you see problems that other people also have?

---

* Many of the ideas in this section are adapted from Neil Taylor and Robin Richardson, *Seeing and Perceiving: Films in a World of Change* (Suffolk, England: Concord Film Council, 1979); and Deborah Barndt, Ferne Cristall and dian marino, *Getting There: Producing Photostories with Immigrant Women* (Toronto: Between The Lines, 1982).

4. **Analysis:** Why does this problem exist? What happens because of it? How does it relate to other problems?

5. **Action:** What resources (person, group, institution, community) could help solve this problem in the short run? In the long run?

Brainstorming

Brainstorming as a technique encourages people to express ideas without self-censoring them or prejudging them. It is a collective activity where everyone pitches in at random to list impressions and ideas. Brainstorming can help solve problems and point out differences and similarities in an audience. Besides opening up discussion it can be a lot of fun.

For example, a group can brainstorm about film images that they liked or did not like — making a list of them — or they could brainstorm about the issues raised or types of people shown in the film. There are no rules for brainstorming but some guidelines are:

1. Record *everyone's* ideas on a flipchart; the more ideas the better.

2. The crazier the better; let imaginations run wild; it sparks creativity and it is fun.

3. Stealing or plagiarism, in this case, is okay; build on other people's ideas, make a variation.

4. Don't evaluate the brainstorm ideas, at least at first; get the ideas out and save the evaluation for later.

After everyone's ideas are recorded, go through the list and decide which ones are most useful to go on talking about.

Listing the Most Vivid Images

This activity is useful in any small group situation. Its purpose is to help viewers focus on the film and look at what they have learned from it.

1. After the film, ask members of the group to write down the images that remain most vivid for them.

2. Have each person pick three important images. "Important" means whatever each person wants it to mean, but if you have to you can define it as meaning the images that most stick out in their minds, or that help them best understand the film.

3. Ask people to pair off and choose what they feel are the three most important images. Roughly sketch images.

4. Pin sketches on a wall and discuss them.

Likes and Dislikes

This quick activity can be useful in bringing people into a discussion. It also helps viewers form opinions and challenge the ideas put forward in the film.

1. Ask each person to write down one thing she liked in the film and one thing she didn't like.

2. Form small groups to discuss this list of points.

Expectations and Reality

This activity gets at stereotyping and can be especially useful for groups with little prior knowledge of the issues. It is most effective in small groups.

1. Before the film starts, give a brief description of the film (name, year, date, where it was made, the issues being addressed).

2. Again before the film, ask participants to jot down what they expect to see and hear. You can prompt answers with questions such as, "What kind of people do you expect to see in the film?" "What do you think they will be wearing?" "What do you think their homes will be like?"

3. After showing the film, discuss similarities or differences between what people expected or did not expect to see, and what they actually saw.

Discussing the Film's Style

This activity raises questions about how a film's style affects its content. Not all of these questions will relate to every film you use.

1. What is the difference between a good lecture and a good documentary?

2. How does the style affect the content? For example, how does the lighting, framing, or music contribute to an understanding of the film?

3. Would you call this a "feminist film"? If so, what makes it so?

4. Are women in the film portrayed differently than in Hollywood films or advertising images? If so, how is this done?

5. Can you see a relationship between the filmmaker and her subjects? Is she observing and distant, or does she interact with them?

6. Does the film make its point of view clear or does it try to be objective?

7. Do women's films contain unique attributes? If so, what are they? If not, why not?

(There's more background information on film style in chapter 4, "Taking A Closer Look at Feminist Filmmaking".)

Creating a Story with Photographs

This activity teaches about the structure of film. It shows how filmmaking is a series of choices, not an objective activity. Editing (or the act of arranging images and sound in sequence and combination) is a technical activity that clearly affects the content of the film.

1. Bring about six to ten photographs (some close-ups, medium, and long shots). If possible bring a number of copies of each.

2. Break into small groups, and place the photos in a sequence on a large sheet of paper. Write in words and sounds on the paper to go with the photos.

3. In your small group, talk about why you decided to place the photos in a particular order.

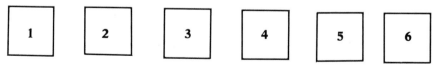

Audience evaluation

It is often awkward to initiate evaluations of the showing and discussion but they are useful: both to participants, so they can consider what they have just seen or learned; and to a discussion leader, to help her assess her own role and the overall success of the event. A good way to do an evaluation is to pass out a form to people as they come into the event. The form can then be quickly filled out and returned at the end of the showing.

Sample Evaluation One

This questionnaire can be used to assess a discussion of any audio-visual showing. To show their views, participants would circle the numbers in the middle of the page. For example, if they completely agree with the statement on the left of the page, and not at all with the one opposite, they would circle number 1. If they think the truth is halfway between the two statements, they would circle number 3, etc.

Title of Film, Video, or Event _____

Group and Location _____

Date _____

The Film

The issues were presented in a confusing way.	1 2 3 4 5	The issues were clear.
The style was boring.	1 2 3 4 5	The style was stimulating.
Music and sound effects didn't contribute much.	1 2 3 4 5	Music/sound effects were powerful, enhancing the experience of the film.
The content was not informative.	1 2 3 4 5	The content was informative.
The film was not entertaining.	1 2 3 4 5	The film was entertaining.

The Discussion

I didn't learn anything new.	1 2 3 4 5	I learned a lot.
Participation was poor; only a few people spoke.	1 2 3 4 5	Participation was good; everyone felt free to speak.
Debate was poor; little critical discussion of each other's views.	1 2 3 4 5	Debate was good; issues were discussed in a thorough way.
Not an interesting discussion.	1 2 3 4 5	A very interesting discussion.
The outcome wasn't useful; group didn't have a clearer understanding at the end.	1 2 3 4 5	Outcome was useful; the group achieved a better understanding of the topic.

Sample Evaluation Two

Title of Film, Video, or Event _____

Group and Location _____

Date _____

1. What did you find most useful? (Both in the film and in the discussion)

2. What would you change?

3. What other comments and suggestions do you have?

4. Would you like to continue working on this subject? If so, please leave your name, address, and phone number in the space below.

Organizing Public Showings

The increasing number of women's film festivals and series is a tribute to the range of films now available and to the varied and complex expressions of women filmmakers. Women's films are drawing large and receptive audiences — an indication not only of growing interest but also of the importance of exhibiting the films. The showings provide cultural, artistic, and educational programs that would otherwise be unavailable.

It is becoming more and more apparent that women organizing

showings of women's culture is one way of taking control over our lives and developing pride in our achievements, awareness of our histories, our futures, and our present situations.

These large public showings of women's film differ from small-group showings in several ways. Small-group screenings tend to happen with a somewhat familiar group of people who at the least share common concerns, if not common viewpoints. Public showings most often aim at larger, more "unknown" audiences. They require more and different kinds of publicity, and call for a different kind of setting: an auditorium or a movie theatre, perhaps, rather than a small meeting room.

For a large public showing you probably need to charge admission to cover your costs. With good publicity, the event can also be a fundraiser. Your costs are going to be higher and you need a detailed budget. To deal with all of this detail you need a strong core of organizers who both work efficiently as individuals and are well co-ordinated as a group.

Many of the aspects and guidelines that we've outlined for small-group screenings also apply to organizing a public event, and it helps to be familiar with them. At the same time, a large public showing involves complex organizing tasks. It can seem that every day brings a need for coping with fresh problems, new decisions.

The many different jobs to be done and choices to be made require a firm sense of control and direction. A series of checklists can help as you follow the rather intricate route through selecting and designing the program, to finding a location for the screening, to building a budget and doing promotion and publicity.

Organizing Tasks: A Checklist

Note: It might be useful to photocopy these pages of the book so you can have them handy when you go about organizing your event.

1. *The Event Itself*

- Define your goals.
- Define your intended audience.
- Decide on whether it will be a single event or a series.
- Make your final choice of films.
- Select date and time of event.

- Choose the location.
- Decide whether to charge admission — if so, how much and whether you want to sell tickets in advance, and how you'll do this.

2. *The Film*

- Decide whether the film will be the main focus of the event.
- Decide about speakers and resource people.
- Decide whether to invite the filmmaker, if she is available.
- Decide if you want other cultural events to take place along with the film showing.
- Decide whether to have a discussion afterwards.

3. *The Organizing*

- Determine whether you want to invite another group to co-sponsor the event.
- Set up the decision-making group and structure.
- Decide whether you want an advance screening for the press.
- Look into child care, wheelchair accessibility, and interpretation for the hearing impaired.
- Decide whether to have book or information tables at the event.
- Decide when and how often to meet with the organizing committee.

Work to Be Done: A Checklist

* Denotes activities essential to all public screenings. The necessity of the other activities varies depending on the nature of the event.

1. *In Advance*

- * Book film and arrange shipping.
- * Reserve the viewing space and check that it is set up for screening films and for wheelchair accessibility.
- * Draw up budget.
- * Produce promotional flyer.
- * Distribute promotional materials.
- * Arrange necessary equipment.
- Produce poster.
- Produce promotional material and distribute to media.

45

- Produce or purchase tickets.
- Arrange child care and signer for the deaf.
- Arrange speakers or resource people.
- Contact filmmaker.
- Liaise with community groups.

2. *At the Event*

* • Host the event.
* • Set up and operate the equipment.
* • Set up room.
  • Sell tickets.
* • Co-ordinate sequence of events.
  • Co-ordinate discussion or question-and-answer period.
  • Set up and service booktable.

Establishing a working group

Delegating responsibility for an event's organizational jobs at the beginning helps ensure that the event will proceed smoothly. We list here some of the general areas of work to be considered, and the specific tasks that fall within each of them.

1. *Project Co-ordinator*

a) Maintains an overview of the process.

b) Delegates work to other members or volunteers and ensures that it is carried out.

c) Works with a committee or committees, and sets up meetings, which may include chairing.

d) Books films and arranges shipping.

e) Reserves the viewing space.

f) Contacts the filmmaker (if appropriate).

g) Arranges speakers or resource people.

h) Draws up budget, or sees that a committee or the group delegates someone to do this.

i) Co-ordinates finances (if the group doesn't have a treasurer).

j) Organizes evaluation.

2. *Production of Promotional Materials*

   a) Compile all necessary information for flyers, posters, advertisements, tickets. Include: the name of the film and filmmaker, awards, actors, reviews, synopsis; date and day of showing; location; time; the name of the sponsoring group or groups, or co-sponsors; child-care details; information on wheelchair accessibility. Photographs from the film provide useful images for flyers and posters.

   b) Make up mock designs and have them approved by the group.

   c) Do the final layout and assembly of materials to be printed.

   d) Arrange for printing.

3. *Distribution of Promotional Materials*

   a) Co-ordinate distribution of flyers and posters.

   b) Work with the media (both alternative and mainstream depending on the event).

   c) Organize direct mailings to your community or desired audience.

   d) Inform other community groups and institutions.

   e) Place advertisements in newspapers, magazines, etc.

4. *Technical Co-ordination*

   a) Check on what equipment is required, for example: projector, screen, microphones, loudspeakers, the right-size take-up reel, extra bulbs (for both sound and light), extension cords, scissors, tape.

   b) Arrange for equipment to be delivered and set up.

   c) Ensure that someone is available and able to operate the equipment.

5. *Logistics of Event*

   a) Find someone to act as host for the event.

   b) Co-ordinate the timing of the event, for example, cue the projectionist about when to start, when to get the lights turned out.

   c) Co-ordinate sequence of events: introduction, speakers, cultural presentation, film, discussion.

d) Handle general troubleshooting.

e) Oversee child care: arrange for a room, equipment, toys, workers.

f) Find a signer for the deaf, and make sure she is positioned properly, to be seen by everyone.

g) Arrange booktables and make sure the literature gets there.

h) Organize the background music if desired.

i) Arrange for someone to host of look after the filmmaker or other guests.

When to hold the event

The time of your event should accommodate the schedule of the expected audience. For instance, a late-evening showing won't be suitable for senior citizens, a dinner-hour showing will stop many women with children from attending, and a film in a farming community might run into trouble if it is planned for harvest time.

A way around these kinds of problems is to show the film more than once, which enables you to target a particular audience for a particular showing. It's a good idea to check local community calendars to avoid clashing with the timing of other events.

A Note on Planning a Series

For a series it is usually best to schedule the films to show at a regular time and place, on the same day of each week. This allows people to plan ahead to attend and for momentum to build. For example, you could schedule films for Sunday afternoons at a movie theatre or for noon-hours at a workplace. Spreading film showings out over a long period of time can give people more opportunity to see each film and also not be overloaded with information all at once.

Where to hold the event

When choosing a location for the event, consider your target audience, your goals, and the available budget. Try to find a place that is known and accessible to the audience you want to attract. Do not, for example, have an evening showing at a location on a dark street.

If you are not using a movie theatre or a hall that is set up for regular showings, make sure the room you have is suitable for film screenings. Check that:

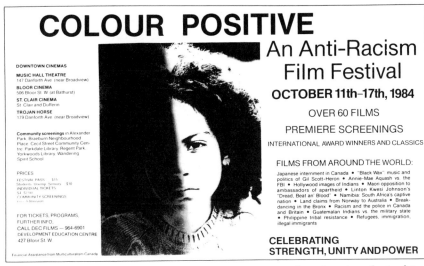

A poster from the first English language international anti-racism festival in Canada. Co-ordinated by DEC Films, October 1984

a) There are enough chairs.

b) There is a power source (and extension cord if necessary) for the projector.

c) The room can be blacked out for daytime showings.

d) The space is big enough for the anticipated audience.

e) There is something to project the film onto: a screen, white wall, clean white sheet, or white canvas.

f) There is someone to open up and lock up, if necessary.

g) It is easy to get to by transit or car.

h) It is wheelchair accessible.

Movie Theatres

Advantages: Access to movie theatres for showing films is not always easy or necessary, but there are some advantages. The projection systems are usually good and there are experienced projectionists. The seating arrangements don't interfere with the projection, and people are used to going to theatres to see films. There are usually

49

refreshments available from a concessions booth and room in the lobby for book tables. A note of caution: most theatres have 35mm projectors, and not all have 16mm projectors, so you'll have to check on this.

Disadvantages: Theatres are usually costly to rent and not always available. They require professional projectionists whose fees are high. Some theatre chains arrange their programming far in advance and do not offer access to outsiders. Independently-owned and -operated theatres are the best bet for renting.

Check whether the theatre is available during "off" times such as weekend days or weeknights early in the week. The cost might be substantially less. If the owner is sympathetic to your goals, you might be able to make arrangements to share expenses and split income. Theatres might not have extra rooms available so you might have to find space somewhere else nearby for child care. Another potential problem is that if the theatre turns out to be too large for your expected audience, you could find yourselves drowning a good turnout in a sea of empty seats.

Community Halls

Advantages: Community halls are likely to cost less than theatres and the people who run them are probably used to dealing with community groups and small organizations. You might also be able to find a hall located right in the community you are trying to reach. It might be a familiar setting where people are used to attending events.

Disadvantages: You could have to take your own equipment and set up the room for a screening, and the sound could be bad. Places with high ceilings and hard walls tend to muffle or distort sound (a problem often posed by churches) unless they have a good public address or speaker system.

Public Libraries

Advantages: Libraries are usually easy to get to and often have a screening room or meeting place available for community organizations. They are either free of charge or have a low rental fee. The library might also be interested in promoting the event to its membership.

Disadvantages: Libraries do not usually allow groups to charge an entrance fee (although it could be okay to pass the hat). If your showing ends after the library's regular closing time, you will need to make special arrangements for keeping it open. Be prepared to pay an overtime fee to cover the library's extra cost for overtime supervision. One other potential problem could be room size: library meeting rooms tend to be small.

University or College Auditoriums

Advantages: University or college auditoriums have fixed seats and, quite often, screens and projection facilities either built-in or accessible through the media departments. If you want to reach a student audience this could be a good location. Rental fees vary, but you might get a reduction if someone in the group is a student or teacher at the school. Student groups often have budgets that allow them to cover costs or get costs waived by the university. You might benefit from this if you arrange for a student group to co-sponsor the event with you.

Disadvantages: People in your target audience might find a university or college setting intimidating and unfamiliar. The campus is also sometimes difficult to get to.

Galleries and Cultural Centres

Advantages: Local art galleries and cultural centres sometimes co-sponsor film events with community groups, or rent out their spaces for showings. The policy and cost vary considerably from one place to the next (many don't charge at all). Consider co-sponsorship with a gallery or centre, especially if you intend to invite a Canadian filmmaker — because you might then be eligible for government funding (from the Canada Council, for instance).

Disadvantages: You might have to provide your own equipment. Again, it needs to be a location and atmosphere that is convenient and familiar — inviting — to your target audience.

It takes considerable time and probably some money to have a filmmaker attend the screening of her film. But it can be worth it for the additional publicity as well as the educational and entertainment value of her presence. A "host" person should be assigned to look

Inviting and engaging the filmmaker

51

after the filmmaker during her stay. This doesn't have to be one person, just so long as someone is always ready to take her around and help her get through her schedule. Don't forget to allow some quiet, relaxed time for the filmmaker, time for her to get off by herself if she wants. It is better to have an energetic and fresh filmmaker part of the time than an exhausted one all the time.

For some events you can apply to the Canada Council for a grant to invite a Canadian filmmaker to show her film in your community. This applies especially to situations where the filmmaker's presence at your showing works in conjunction with a workshop for local film producers, where you are having a retrospective of her work, or where the showing is curated by a local gallery or cultural centre. The Council encourages public showings of Canadian films and videos, and welcomes inquiries. Its address is: Canada Council, Media Arts, P.O. Box 1047, Ottawa, Ont. K1P 5V8, phone (613) 237-3400.

Preparing a budget

A group does not necessarily need a great deal of money to show films publicly. There are some sources of free films across the country, including the government-sponsored National Film Board (NFB) and public libraries (although if you charge admission, the NFB films are not free). Independent film distributors have to charge a rental fee and they usually return about 50 per cent of the fee to the filmmaker. Rental fees and other expenses affect your decision about whether to charge admission and how much, but don't let them scare you off.

The following budget outlines show the range of expenses you can expect and the specific categories to take into account.

General Budget for a Public Showing

Expense Items	Notes on Cost
Theatre or Hall	Free, to several hundred dollars for a public location.
Promotion	
Flyers & Posters	Range from $15 to $400 depending on the design and number you choose to print. Costs include typesetting, letraset, photostats, photocopying, and printing. Coloured ink and coloured paper cost a bit extra.

Tickets	Depend on whether you produce your own tickets by photocopying, or buy commercially produced tickets.
Advertising	Includes artwork plus a charge for running the ad in various publications, from community newspapers to the mainstream press depending on your budget and the desired audience.
Press Kits	An original press kit might be available for free from the distributor. There may be additional costs for photocopying or photo reproduction.
Film Rental and Shipping	The person or group renting a film pays for the shipping cost, which can sometimes be as much as the film rental. Ask the distributor to estimate the amount. Include additional shipping costs for preview, if necessary. Film rental costs, if any, vary according to the length of the film and the policies of the distributor.
Equipment Rental	Projectors and video machines are sometimes available for free from school boards or libraries. Commercial rental prices vary. Include costs of microphones, speakers, extension cords, etc., and of transporting the equipment to and from the event.
Speakers and Resource People	Include honoraria and transportation expenses. There could be huge variations depending on the individual and the negotiations.
Appearance by the Filmmaker	This can run to hundreds of dollars (including travel, honorarium, and per diem expenses). Canadian filmmakers might be able to apply for Canada Council funding to help.
Postage	For mailing flyers, press kits, and any correspondence.

53

Miscellaneous	Include long-distance phone calls, gas, couriers, and a contingency fund.
Refreshments	Often a way to make extra money — or you can serve them free, in which case they will be an extra cost.

Some Cost-Cutting Hints:

- For a good cause — especially a benefit showing — a lot of people are willing to help out. So try to organize as much volunteer help as possible.
- Someone with access to a photocopier at work might be able to produce flyers and press kits.
- Volunteers are often interested in doing the phone calls and the running around that are a part of promotion.
- A volunteer might offer to drive her or his car around to distribute flyers or to pick up the films.
- Sympathetic businesses can donate goods and services, thus cutting costs and helping to increase income. (Financial donations should be acknowledged whenever possible and appropriate, in publicity and promotional material.)
- By all means, use your contacts and build up a labour pool to help out in whatever way possible.

Admission Price

If you need to charge for the film you might want to set a reduced price for low-income people (senior citizens, unemployed, single mothers, students). You might be tempted to charge a lower price in general to draw more people, although this should be balanced against the importance of valuing women's films properly even if they are not well known or commercially-made. People usually expect to pay something to see a film, so be careful not to undervalue the showing.

Note: Income can be raised from sources other than ticket sales; for example, from donations by endorsing groups of the community, and from grants.

SAMPLE BUDGETS
For Public Showings of a Feature Film

	One Premiere Showing *A Small Town in Manitoba*	Three Premiere Showings *A Large City in Ontario*
Cinema or Hall Rental	$25.00	$900.00
Promotion		
Flyers	$15.00	$375.00
Tickets	$ 3.00	$ 30.00
Ads	—	$180.00
Press Kits	—	$ 60.00
Film Rental	$125.00	$375.00
Shipping (both ways)	$ 40.00	pick-up
Filmmaker		
Travel	—	$350.00
Honorarium	—	$150.00
Living Expenses	—	$100.00
Telephone	$ 8.00	$ 75.00
Additional Resource People (honorarium & travel)	—	$ 75.00
Postage	$ 10.00	$ 70.00
Refreshments	$ 15.00	—
Miscellaneous	$ 10.00	$ 50.00
Total Expenses	$251.00	$2790.00

Income
(Example for Break-Even Point)

Ticket Sales:	38 @ $4.50 = $171.00	380 @ $5.00 = $1900.00
	* 20 @ $3.00 = $ 60.00	255 @ $3.50 = $ 892.50
Total	58 tickets = $231.00	635 tickets = $2792.50
Refreshments	$ 20.00	
Total Income	$251.00	$2792.50

* Unemployed, student, or senior citizen price.

Tickets

You can produce your own or purchase ready-made tickets. Advance ticket sales help with cash flow and are an excellent way to get members of the group actively involved in promoting the event to their networks. Tickets need to have film title, time of showing, location, date, and price on them. If there is more than one showing, consider using different coloured tickets for different shows. Advance ticket sales help build an audience. People talk about where they are going and the word of mouth helps draw more of a crowd. At the same time advance ticket sales are more work to co-ordinate.

Promoting the event

The type and amount of promotion you do can make or break your event. It is time-consuming but not difficult, and you will find that if you and your group show enthusiasm for what's happening, the spirit will rub off on other people.

1. Word of Mouth:

Promotion by word of mouth works. If the group is enthusiastic, the word will spread. This means talking about the event to everyone you know and spreading the word to community groups, schools, and institutions.

2. Endorsements:

Endorsements expand the base of support for an event. Your group's request for endorsement from other groups can be based on asking those groups to:

a) Support an issue, e.g., endorsing a film on the right to safe abortion.

b) Support an event, e.g., a film to celebrate International Women's Day.

c) Support an action, e.g., a film showing to raise money for opening a rape crisis centre in the community.

d) Support aims and objectives as differentiated from the film itself. For example, some organizations will be unwilling to endorse a film event without prior screening of the film, but would endorse the aims and objectives of the event.

It is important to make your request for endorsement clearly and in writing. Be sure to:

high schools as your labour pool will allow. There could be competition for space on the more well-used boards, so yours might be taken down or covered over. Have someone retrace the steps to make sure the posters are still visible a few days before the event.

b) *Meetings/Community Events:* Distributing flyers at community meetings and events (or getting other people connected with these meetings to distribute them for you) is a good way to reach various networks. It's also not a bad idea to carry flyers with you wherever you go in the weeks before your own event; you never know when you'll come up with new places to hand them out, or new people to help.

c) *Mailings:* Direct mail is an effective way to reach people, especially if you have a reliable and up-to-date mailing list. Also, find out if other related or sympathetic groups or organizations are doing mailings before your event, and see if they'll include your flyer. This method of "piggybacking" mailings will get your flyers out at a lower cost.

d) *Newsletters:* Sometimes people working on community newsletters will insert flyers in the newsletter itself. If this is not possible, place an announcement in the "community calendar" listings.

e) *Outside postering:* Postering outside may have to be done more than once, because flyers get torn down or destroyed by weather. Try to poster in key areas about two weeks before your event, and then again just a few days before. Use staple guns for postering on wood or other soft surfaces and tape or glue for metal surfaces. To poster large cities, it is advisable to set up key postering routes, using a map of the city to keep track of which routes are covered. If the film is controversial you might want to consider carefully exactly *where* you put your poster.

The ideal in working on any event is to get as much free publicity as you can. And it can be amazing — and exciting — to see just how much free coverage you can stir up.

Remember, all reviews are useful in drawing attention to the event. Even a "bad" review draws attention to the fact that something is happening and to the issues — and doesn't necessarily stop

a) State whether you are seeking endorsement for an issue, an event, an action, or your own group's aims and objectives.

b) Request permission to use the endorsing group's name on any promotional material associated with the event.

c) Request a financial contribution if required or appropriate.

d) Request participation in publicity or selling tickets in advance. You will probably need to follow the letter with a telephone call to supply further information and find out when you can expect to get a decision. Obtaining endorsement from a larger institution can be a lengthy process when approval has to be sought through the various decision-making levels, so allow plenty of time. You will find that when one organization endorses an event it becomes easier for others to follow suit.

3. Producing Flyers and Posters:

a) Gather all the necessary information and write any additional copy. Include:
   name • issue • place • address • time • day • date • price • co-sponsoring group(s) • endorsements • awards • child care • special guests • phone number for more information • brief description of the film • brief description of the sponsoring group • ticket outlets • wheelchair accessibility

b) Design the flyer or poster and have it approved.

c) Do the final layout.

d) Have it printed.

Some Design Tips

- Keep the design simple and not cluttered.
- Too many different type styles make flyers/posters look messy and hard to read.
- Highlight the most important information (name of film, time, day, date, location).
- Keep the description of the film brief, bringing out the most important points.

- If you have both a flyer and a poster, make sure there is a similarity in the design so people will associate both with the event.

- If your budget permits, you may want to have your flyer and/or poster typeset. Phototypesetting is the most common, and any professional type shop can explain the process to you and estimate how much your job will cost. Copy should be cleanly typed, double-spaced. The typesetter can assist you in marking up the copy (specifying size of type, type style, etc.).

- If you cannot afford typesetting for a flyer or poster, and you don't have a lot of copy, pressure transfer lettering (such as Letraset, Geotype, Mecanorama) can be used to make attractive headings. Entire posters can be done in this way, or the headings can be combined with typewritten body copy. Some word processing machines or personal computers produce quite acceptable type, some near to typeset-quality. If you have access to such equipment, you can produce smart-looking work at a very low cost.

A flyer is usually a single sheet of 8½" x 11" or 8½" x 14" paper. Posters are often simply enlargements of the flyer, and a flyer can be a reduction of the poster. Use the posters for display in public places, and use the flyers for display, mailing, and leafletting purposes.

Sometimes the film's distributor already has flyers and posters that will readily adapt to your needs. This may save a lot of work and some expense. However, it is also useful to learn how to make a flyer.

Some Printing Tips

- It is cheaper to print in quantity.

- Check prices at your local copy shop. Photocopying may be cheaper than printing for quantities of less than 500.

- Printing in more than one colour is expensive. A cheaper alternative may be to have the flyer printed on coloured paper (but make sure it is easy to read) or in coloured ink, for only a small extra charge.

- "Instant printing", a printing process that uses paper printing plates, will usually give you decent quality reproductions more cheaply than the process that uses metal plates. A really

Three different posters advertising women's film events. 'Still Ain't on TV' is a simple line drawing in black and white; clear to read and cheap to print. The 'Lifesize' poster is used for an ongoing women's film series with the time and location constant. The program is listed in the empty space. 'Cinémama' is an attractive, professionally designed, and more costly poster to produce. (The original is a three-colour poster.) The cartoon is its main feature with the specific details less prominent.

high quality poster with photographs or two or more colours will probably require a metal plate process.

4. Distributing Flyers/Posters:

Try to line up as many volunteers to help as possible: postering with other people is fun. If possible, have someone co-ordinate the timing of the postering and the locations you want to cover.

a) *Postering Inside:* This involves putting up flyers or posters on public notice boards about two weeks before the event. You should try to cover as many restaurants, stores, community centres, university campuses, bookstores, public libraries, and

people from attending. It is possible, for instance, that a review could be written by a man who has trouble with the issues raised, or fails to see the importance of them, but it is likely that many readers will detect the bias and still want to come and see for themselves.

1. The first step is to make up a list of the various newspapers and magazines that could possibly review, announce, or advertise your event. Find out and list their deadline dates. Your press list should include both mainstream and alternative press, radio and TV, church and campus newspapers, and community newspapers or newsletters. It should include any special interest publications related to the issue or issues connected with the film showing. When available, include on your list the name of a contact person who you think might be interested in or sympathetic to the issue being explored.

2. Try to make direct contact, either in person or by phone, with sympathetic people in the media. This direct contact is sometimes the only way to get the event covered by the press.

3. Make up press releases to send to all the people on your media list. Press releases are written descriptions or "stories" about your event and should briefly outline the contents of the film and its importance, with some information about the sponsoring group. It should if possible use a "news hook" (also known as a peg or angle) connecting your event and its issue to a current news story. (We discuss this more below, in "Working with the Mainstream Media".) Sometimes your press release will be used verbatim by the media while other times the information could be used in a longer article. The press release is the way the media will first hear of the film event, and it can lead to further coverage.

   The elements of a press release are: the date of the release, with "FOR IMMEDIATE RELEASE" typed in the top left-hand corner; a headline of four to six words; a double-spaced story about the film and event, containing pertinent information about time, date, and location; and an identification of the sponsoring group.

4. You might want to compile a press kit to send out with the press release. This does not have to be glossy — press kits are simply packages of promotional material to provide more detailed, lengthy information about the event. They are especially useful

61

when you don't have a personal contact. They can include a synopsis of the film, reviews, a list of awards, a biography of the filmmakers, the flyer, the name and phone number of a contact person, and, if possible, a photograph from the film to be used for publication. Distributors will usually supply you with this material.

5. Follow up by telephone as soon as you think the press release or press kit has arrived. It helps to make sure the material has been received, and to refreshen memories, and see if any further information is required.

6. You might need to make up a different press release for the alternative press, emphasizing more directly or forcefully the issues covered by the showing or the objectives of your group.

7. You might also want or need to have a press screening, an advance showing for the press to encourage a review or article before the event happens. Give notice of this in your press release, and hold the screening in an accessible, central location, with someone from the group to answer questions and supply information. Be prepared to hand out extra press kits if necessary. It is also a good idea to provide refreshments for the people who attend.

   The right time to hold a screening for the daily media is about a week before the film showing. You don't want an article to appear so early that the event gets forgotten. But if the screening is held too late you could miss a deadline. Weekly or monthly publications usually require more lead time. You will need a print or a preview video-cassette from the distributor for the screening.

   Be prepared to set up additional screenings for people who can't make it for the scheduled one (assuming you have the print or video available for this).

Working with the Alternative Media

Because the mainstream media are often not receptive to community events (especially in large cities), many groups find that their energies are much better spent working with the alternative media — university, church, and community or weekly newspapers, newsletters, and magazines as well as campus and community radio stations and cable TV stations. It is encouraging to see how effective these media can be in reaching people, and it is a mistake to think that only high profile, mainstream publicity is useful.

Community newspapers are often staffed by volunteers, so it can be difficult for them to cover the event. If you are having a press screening, be prepared to be flexible in setting up alternative viewing times for people who can't make it to the scheduled time-slot.

Public Service Announcements

Many local newspapers, radio, and TV stations provide space or time for free public service announcements. These are short, concise announcements of community events written in clear and simple language likely to attract listeners' or readers' attention. They should include time, date, location, and cost of the event, along with brief details on the film and the names of the sponsoring groups and any special guests. Make sure the announcements arrive at the appropriate desk at least two weeks before the event, and follow up with phone calls to make sure they see the light of day.

```
            LATINO

PUBLIC SERVICE ANNOUNCEMENT


        Announcing the Toronto premiere showing of
LATINO, a controversial feature film about the
US sponsored contra war against Nicaragua.
        Acclaimed Director/Cinematographer Haskell
Wexler has received several Academy Awards for his
work in such films as Coming Home, One Flew Over The
Cuckoo's Nest, In The Heat of The Night, and
Medium Cool.
        Two shows only, Sunday, December 14th at
1:00 and 3:15 p.m., BLOOR CINEMA, 506 Bloor Street
West (at Bathurst).  $5.00 admission.
        Sponsored by Tools for Peace and Canadian Action
for Nicaragua, call 922-0852 or 534-1766.
                    -30-
We thank you for announcing this dramatic film event.
```

Working with the mainstream media

Your ability to get the mainstream media interested in the event depends a great deal on the community you work in, the contacts you have, the luck you have in finding someone sympathetic, and the nature of the event itself.

In general, working with the media requires enthusiasm and assertiveness — you may have to do a lot of pushing to have a journalist cover the film. You need someone in your group who has an interest in or ability for public speaking. You need to make written and personal contact through press releases, telephone follow-ups, and press screenings.

Above all, don't be defensive. Assume that the information is important for their readers or audiences, and that they should be grateful for all the "great copy" you are supplying them with.

People living in smaller centres might have more success in getting the media to cover local events because there is often less competition. However, success again depends on the nature of the event, the politics of the media, the kind of contacts you have, and the competition for space and time.

Often, especially in larger urban centres, journalists will not deal with films that are not showing commercially at a local theatre. This of course cuts out coverage of a lot of interesting events and means that only high-budget, Hollywood-style movies get reviewed. It is important, therefore, to challenge these traditional notions of what is "newsworthy" to enable women's films to get the recognition they deserve.

When approaching journalists, try to pick out an aspect of the film that is of particular interest to your community. For example, if your film features women in non-traditional work, remind the journalists of the recent affirmative action policy passed to guarantee equal employment opportunities for women. In other words, you might have to spell out why the film is important for the community as a whole and why the media should cover it. This is the news hook you look for in your press release.

In the case of the media, dogged persistence usually pays off. And so does creativity in your approaches. A little opportunism, and a little luck, also help. Don't be discouraged if you get turned away or turned down or simply ignored. The struggle is worthwhile and your successes, when they come, will create the exposure needed to draw out a good audience and make the way easier for the next time around.

Within the mainstream media you'll want to approach as many different forms as you can: TV, radio, newspapers, and the advertising channels.

1. TV Publicity

Offer a clip of the film to TV stations a few days before the event, if they show interest. A clip is a thirty-second to two-minute segment chosen to engage the viewer's interest. If the TV station wants to make a video copy of a 16mm clip, you have to first clear that with the distributor. Usually this will not be a problem because showing a clip provides good promotion for the distributor as well as for you. Make sure the station does not literally cut out and tape back in a piece of the film. Try also to arrange an interview with either the filmmaker or someone in the sponsoring group.

2. Radio Publicity

Try to find radio programs that ordinarily cover the kind of issues dealt with by the film, and see if they will interview a group member or the filmmaker. If you are planning a high profile community event, contact news journalists as well as people producing regular programs such as early morning, noon-hour, or after-four "driving home" programs. Radio stations might also air an audio clip, a thirty-second to two-minute segment of the soundtrack chosen especially to engage interest.

3. Newspaper Publicity

When contacting newspapers, remember to approach the features and news editors as well as film reviewers. Columnists and reporters assigned to special areas (for example, women's health or consumer issues) can be allies in promoting certain events. They will sometimes mention the event and its purpose in their columns. This will reach women who read columns but don't necessarily look at film reviews.

If there is more than one film reviewer, try to figure out which one is most likely to help your cause, and approach her or him first. It is a good idea to supply film reviewers with press kits to help them with background information.

4. Paid Advertising

You might want to take out paid advertisements in selected community newspapers, magazines, or mainstream papers. The cost can be high, varying considerably according to the nature of the publication, its circulation, and the size of the ad. Paid advertisements are often too expensive for smaller community events, but it could prove worthwhile to allocate even a small advertising budget if fundraising is one of your goals and you're concerned about reaching out to new audiences. Try to advertise in the magazines and newspapers that you think are most likely to review the film. That way you can benefit from one of the most important principles in promotion: repetition.

A few more details

1. Child Care

Advertise the availability of child care and have people pre-register for it. Make sure you have a suitable space and enough toys and equipment. Also ensure you have enough people working, at least one of whom has experience.

2. Booktables and Literature

If you want to have tables for showing literature, selling books, buttons, or posters, or even simply keeping a mailing list to sign, find out whether there are tables available at the location of the event or if you will have to supply them. As well, you will need to arrange for someone to transport the material or literature. If you are planning to sell items, you will need to have a cash box and money-float. It is often a good idea to have a brightly coloured cloth on the table to make the display more attractive. You should also decide whether you can accommodate book and information tables by other groups: You might get requests.

3. Sequence of Events

Don't overload the program — let people leave feeling full of energy, not exhausted. Be clear about the order of introductions, talk, readings, the film, discussion (if there is one), and closing. Decide whether to make community announcements: Again, you're likely to get requests for these, possibly at the last minute.

Evaluation and follow-up

Assessing the group's programming and publicity after the event helps to improve future efforts. You can learn by mistakes as well as successes and now you'll have some concrete experiences to reflect on. Evaluations are meant to be forward-looking — not simply post-mortems and full of regrets. It is useful at the time of the event to write down your impressions for future reference: You'll be surprised at how soon those thoughts slip away afterwards as you take on new projects.

The evaluation of the public showing can come not only from within the group — but also from the audience.

1. You might want to distribute an evaluation form to the audience before the film begins — as people come through the door, for instance — to be filled in and handed in after the showing (see chapter 2, "Audience Evaluation" for sample forms).

2. The working group should meet about a week after the event for an evaluation session.* This provides time for the group to recuperate but means their ideas and criticisms will still be fresh. The evaluation meeting provides a forum for sharing what each person learned as an individual and for identifying the problems, limitations, and mistakes — as well as the successes — as a group. While individuals must be allowed to express their personal opinions, the evaluation session should not focus on "laying blame" but rather on concrete suggestions and group process.

You can break down your evaluation into four areas:

1. The Film

- Was it appropriate (in style, length, subject, approach, content, quality)?
- Did it generate the response you anticipated?
- Did it match your goals?
- Did it cover the issues?

2. The Audience

- Who came?
- How many people came? Were there more or less than expected?

---

* This evaluation process is adapted from Linda Blackaby, Dan Georgakas and Barbara Margolis, *In Focus: A Guide to Using Films* (New York: Zoetrpoe, 1980).

- Did you reach your expected target audience?
- Were there any surprises at the showing?
- What was the audience's response?

3. Program Format

- Was it a good choice of time, date, and location?
- Did the sequence of events run smoothly?
- Were the speaker and cultural events appropriate to the film?
- Was the discussion lively, engaging? How much did the audience participate?
- What things about the event were most successful? What was least successful?

4. The Group

- Did you meet your goals?
- Were you effective in planning and organizing?
- Was there enough time to carry out all of the planning tasks?
- Did people carry out their responsibilities?
- How effective was the publicity? Which of the methods you used were most successful? Which were least successful?
- How thorough was the community outreach?
- Are there any interpersonal tensions that need to be resolved?
- Are you within budget? Are expenses and income different from what you projected? Why is that?
- Did the decision-making process work?

5. Future Projects and Ongoing Work

- What are the implications of your evaluation for future projects and ongoing work?

Finally, at the end of the evaluation session, you should decide what follow-up needs to be done: for example, writing thank you letters; passing on the evaluations to the filmmakers and resource people;

incorporating all the new contacts into your mailing list and media file; doing a final report to a funding agency, if necessary.

One further note: the scraps of paper you have probably been using all this time to make notes as the event developed and unfolded might make sense now but they are unlikely to mean much — or will be lost — by the time the next event comes around and you have to start planning once more. So a final, eventually rewarding step is to take time as soon as possible after the showing to organize the various bits of information into a coherent form — and to file it all away in a place where you can easily find it later on, when you need it again.

And don't forget to go out and celebrate.

CHAPTER

4

Taking a Closer Look at Feminist Filmmaking

Women artists create images in poetry, prose, painting, sculpture, film, and video, images that reflect their life experiences. At the same time, many women artists have been positively influenced by, if not involved in, the women's movement over recent decades. And it is the films and videos by these artists in particular that we term "feminist film".

71

And so I came home a woman starving
for images
to say my hunger is so old
so fundamental, that all the lost
crumbled burnt smashed shattered defaced
overpainted concealed and falsely named
faces of every past we have searched together
in all ages
could rise reassemble re-collect re-member themselves. . . .

I am remembered by you, remember you
even as we are dismembered
on the cinema screens. . . .

This is the war of the images
We are the thorn leaf guarding the purple-tongued flower
each to each.

— Adrienne Rich

Our view of feminist film here is expansive rather than concise and restrictive. It reflects some of the contradictions and difficulties, the varieties and possibilities, apparent within the women's movement itself. Women filmmakers are not a cohesive group. They take up different issues, come from diverse cultures, have varying ideologies, and use a multitude of film forms. Yet there is common ground among women filmmakers. They are concerned with making themselves heard and seen as women, and they value the knowledge gained from women's experiences.

Still, it is difficult to pin-point specifically what unites feminist filmmakers. Women artists talk about a "feminine language" — a way that women express what is in their hearts and minds differently from men. Some feminist film critics discuss how women filmmakers disrupt the dominant pattern of images of women — a pattern that reflects male fantasies and is rarely true to women's experiences.* As a result, consciously or unconsciously, feminist films are most often made in opposition to the dominant cinema — that is, the films of Hollywood or mainstream North America. They are sometimes called "oppositional" or "counter" cinema.

But it is complicated. Belgian filmmaker Chantal Ackerman says:

It's really a hard problem to say what differentiates a woman's rhythm in film because a man can use the same forms of expression.

* See "Women and Film: A Discussion of Feminist Aesthetics," *New German Critique* No. 13, 1978.

I don't know if we have the words, if they exist yet. We speak of 'women's rhythm' but it isn't necessarily the same for all women. I also think that Hollywood doesn't express a man's rhythm either, but the rhythm of Capitalism. . . . Men are cheated by it too.*

20TH CENTURY FOX

Feminists from all cultural backgrounds are alike in that they critique the "product" of Hollywood. U.S. film critic Molly Haskell writes:

> The big lie perpetrated on Western Society is the idea of women's inferiority, a lie so deeply ingrained in our social behavior that merely to recognize it is to risk unraveling the entire fabric of civilization. . . . In the movie business, we have had an industry dedicated for the most part to reinforcing the lie.†

The spectacle of high-budget Hollywood movies — engrossing

---

* *OTHER CINEMA*, Women's Catalogue, London, England, 1980.

† Molly Haskell, *From Reverence to Rape: The Treatment of Women in the Movies* (New York: Holt, Rinehart & Winston, 1974), pp. 1-2.

stories, beautiful photography, sensational special effects, action-packed dramas, out-of-this-world fantasies, famous movie stars — attracts millions of people to the theatres every year. Even with the advent of television in the 1950s and the growing home video industry of the 1980s, people have continued to go out to the movies. While the great emotional impact of watching a film on a big screen is still a main attraction, movie-going is also a social activity, a part of cultural life in cities and towns, especially for the young.

Since the early 1970s, feminist film critics have looked closely at the variety of roles Hollywood has created for women: roles that include sex goddess, faithful wife, vamp, and "girl friday". They have concluded that most roles for women in Hollywood movies are limited and stereotypical, not only in their depiction of women's experience, but also in who is depicted. In the first place, almost exclusively, famous actresses are white — from Lillian Gish, Mae West, Jean Harlow, Bette Davis, Lauren Bacall, and Marilyn Monroe to contemporary stars such as Jane Fonda, Meryl Streep, Bo Derek, and Sally Field. Women of colour rarely appear in major roles and they are even more scarce than white women in the fields of scriptwriting and directing.

A few women directors, such as Claudia Weill (*Girlfriends*), Lee Grant (*Tell Me A Riddle*), and Susan Seidelman (*Desperately Seeking Susan*) have been allowed to work on Hollywood films. They are exceptions to the rule. Hollywood does not have a good record. Film critic Irene Wolt found, "Of the 7,332 feature films released from 1949 to 1979, only 14 were directed by women." Although the 1980s have brought some changes, according to Irene Wolt women remain drastically "underrepresented in all creative positions in the industry. In 1983 female directors accounted for only two percent of the days worked on feature films. Fewer than fifteen percent of all the feature films made from April 1982 to April 1983 were written by women."*

In the last decade Hollywood has recognized and responded to the influence of the women's movement by making films that focus on strong women, showing their growing independence and desire to take power over their lives. The films *Norma Rae* and *Nine To Five* (both of them directed by men) illustrate the strengths and weaknesses of this trend.

Mae West

* Irene Wolt, "All Dressed Up With No Place To Go," *American Film*, Vol. 10, No. 3.

From Girlfriends *directed by Claudia Weill*

Norma Rae is about a woman with a sense of growing anger about unfair and dangerous working conditions in the garment factory where she works. As a result she becomes a rank-and-file union organizer. It is exhilarating to watch a movie where the heroine is a mother and a factory worker, a strong and compassionate woman. But the film shows Norma Rae as an exceptional heroine among working-class women. She has more meaningful contact with an out-of-town, middle-class union organizer than with her working-class women friends and co-workers.

Nine To Five was based on research done with the organization of U.S. women office workers of the same name. Using comedy, it taps the creative imagination of women who fantasize about controlling their workplace and hanging the boss by his heels from the ceiling. *Nine To Five* is witty and fun and brings women together in laughter and common concerns about office work. But it blames the terrible working conditions almost exclusively on the boss. The solution is to get rid of him, paint the walls, allow a woman to become boss, and be happy. The movie offers no serious appraisal of women's work. It does not examine concrete — as opposed to fantastic — ways to change the

WARNER BROS. INC.

Sally Field in Norma Rae *by Martin Ritt*

From Nine to Five

power structure in an office, nor does it look at the importance of unions or women's organizations in making changes.*

Hollywood definitely sets up "acceptable limits" of social criticism, and the fantasies and fears in these films must adhere to financial concerns and production policies — both determined by men. No Hollywood film about women can call for a serious disruption of social order, and most still feature extreme and frequently violent sexism. The room given to women's issues is shaped, decorated, and populated almost exclusively by men. The "women's films" are filled with opposing and contradictory messages that continue to depict women as sex objects, victims, or bound to traditional roles, and show women's problems as petty and individual rather than as major issues in society. At the same time they totally ignore the very existence of huge numbers and whole groups of women.

But for all these shortcomings some films, such as *Norma Rae*, and *Nine To Five*, or more recently *Coal Miner's Daughter* and *The Color Purple* do portray women as appealing role models, women who

---

* This interpretation is indebted to Carol Slingo, "9 to 5: Blondie gets the Boss", in *JUMPCUT: A Review of Contemporary Cinema*, No. 24/25, p. 1.

celebrate our strengths and leave us feeling full of new energy. They can provide enjoyable entertainment and give room to women's fantasies.

Hollywood's "women's films", though, are far from ideal. And it is clear that Hollywood has responded to the women's movement by producing such films not because the movie industry has had a change of ideology — the numerous other sexist films make this obvious — but because the women's movement is a large and potentially profitable movie-going market.

> From the start, its link to an evolving political movement gave feminist cinema a power and direction entirely unprecedented in independent filmmaking, bringing issues of theory/practice, aesthetics/meaning, process/representation into sharp focus.*

Although Hollywood and the women's movement are unlikely partners, because of their differing approaches to presenting women's issues they have both had a major impact on feminist filmmaking. For many women filmmakers, Hollywood sparked the critique and the notion of what women are not, while the women's movement generated the courage to create alternative images of what women are and can be.

Within the diversity of the women's movement it has always been important, when working on issues of common concern, to recognize points of unity. These points include the concept of the personal as political and a commitment to a process based on feminist principles. The principles stress making room for open and equal participation and exchange in order to air and clarify ideas, concepts, tensions, and contradictions. Such attributes of the women's movement have clearly influenced feminist film productions.

Watching a woman do dishes or sweep a floor, hearing women discuss their emotions around childbearing or post-partum depression, or seeing women behind huge machines: These are relatively new images for the film screen. Previously, when these issues have been addressed it has most often been through a male writer or narrator or through institutional or government analysis. Women filmmakers document women's lives from a woman's point of view.

Movies and the women's movement

JOHN PHILLIPS

From Yes We Can *by Laura Sky*

---

* B. Ruby Rich, "In The Name of Feminist Film Criticism", *JUMP CUT: Hollywood, Politics and Counter-Cinema*, ed. Peter Steven, (Toronto: Between The Lines, 1985) pp. 210-211.

77

Women filmmakers have highlighted the concept of the personal as political in new ways. The direct impact of film allows filmmakers to explore emotions as they relate to the social fabric of characters' lives through images as well as words, songs, sound effects, and camera angles. For example, fiction directors create characters whose personal changes relate directly to a growing consciousness of women's position in society, while several documentary makers have focused exclusively on women telling their stories to the camera — stories of abuse, poverty, and health, to name a few. Some experimental filmmakers have explored the experience of "space closing in" on a woman isolated in the home.

Also implicit in a feminist approach to process is a critique of hierarchical decision-making structures. This discussion includes questions of filmmaking and the connections between production, distribution, and exhibition. For example:

- What is the filmmaker's relationship to those filmed (that is, collective, collaborative, sympathetic)?
- What power do the subjects have over the final product?
- Who is the audience for the film?
- How will the film be distributed?

Though filmmakers answer these questions differently, few dispute their importance.

A second approach looks at the questions of film viewing, and the ways of understanding a film's point of view. For instance, in a conversation with a friend your response depends on how you are feeling, what your experience of the topic has been, and whether or not you agree with what is being said. You interpret the words and create the meaning of the conversation as you participate in it. Similarly, some feminist critics suggest that because viewers process the ideas put forward in a film through their own understanding of the world, they also give the film its meaning.

Other critics suggest a dialectical relationship between the filmmaker's interpretation of issues and events and the viewer's interpretation of the film. The tension lies between the film and viewer's capacity to create meaning.

Imagine viewing a film with a group of women. In the group there will probably be more than one viewpoint concerning what you have seen. Does this suggest that the filmmaker raises questions without having clearly thought through the subject matter? Or does it indicate that regardless of how clear a filmmaker is about her point of view, the meaning of the film depends on the ideological and cultural perspective of the viewer? Does the film give a mixed message that leads to a confusing discussion? Is it better for a film to take a stand on an issue, to simply raise the questions, or to do both?

These considerations are important for filmmakers and viewers and indicate the interconnections between producer and audience. The questions are not mutually exclusive, but women's positions on them affect the definitions of and approaches to feminist film. They help us to develop our consciousness of how films work and how we understand and react to them.

Positive images

The history of Hollywood offers plenty of examples of stereotyped images: women as "madonnas" or "whores", Native Americans as "red savages", Afro-Americans as "mammies" or "prostitutes". For good reason, women and people of colour (especially women of colour) want to see strong, diverse characters on the screen — "positive images" of themselves. These would be images that challenge stereotypes, focus on specific concerns, and document their contributions throughout history.

It is no easy task to challenge the media's portrayal of racist and sexist attitudes and to explode the social myths that provide the foundation for those attitudes. Nor is it an easy task to create positive images in a world where women's experiences are often far from positive. Sometimes positive images are defined by their closeness to real life experience; other times, they are defined by their affirming, progressive, and forward-looking portrayal of people's situations.*

A view of life showing "things as they really are" is a feature of the documentary film *It's Not Your Imagination,* where five women from different economic backgrounds describe their frustrations and anger about being sexually harassed on the job. The short drama *A Minor Alteration* takes the "things as they should be" approach. It explores racism through the story of a fight between a white girl and

WOMEN IN FOCUS

From It's Not Your Imagination

---

* This idea and much of the following discussion of positive images comes from Diane Waldman, "There's More To A Positive Image Than Meets The Eye," in Peter Steven, ed., *JUMPCUT: Hollywood, Politics and Counter-Cinema* (Toronto: Between The Lines, 1985).

79

From Union Maids *directed by Julia Reichert, James Klein and Miles Mogelescu*

a black girl over a school course that will accept only one of them. The film raises questions about streaming black kids into less skilled, less academic courses, and shows parents angrily confronting the school principal to demand answers and changes.

Though they take startlingly different approaches, both of these films provide tools for challenging stereotypes. It is necessary to recognize those different approaches when looking towards a definition of "positive image".

Similarly, interpretations of positive images vary. One example that raises questions is the role of women in non-traditional occupations. Most women agree, in principle, that images of women in these roles are positive. But factory forewomen, corporate executives, scientists, plumbers, truck drivers, welders, or mechanics cannot easily be lumped together. Some women argue that a corporate executive represents the power establishment, which has always kept women in a second-class position, and that she cannot therefore represent women's interests.

This raises more than the question of role models; it also shows different class interests. Some women will find heroines in the women labour organizers of the 1930s in the film *Union Maids*, or among the Wives Supporting the Strike in *A Wives' Tale*, while others see positive models in professional women, such as the psychiatrist in *A Question of Silence*. This conflict in defining a positive image mirrors conflicts in the women's movement, where women who seek reforms to the present system and ways for women to participate more actively in it are split off from women who seek more radical changes through restructuring the economic system.

No amount of positive image-making will alone undermine the power of the dominant media's "negative images". Whether a film's images are positive or negative, it is necessary to go beyond those labels to study and discuss their content, meanings, ideology, and message. It is when women use films to explore issues in a critical way that we challenge the roots of sexist attitudes and gain new insights. Positive images must not just be accepted as "good" over either "evil" or "negative images". A close look at the most dynamic and inspiring portrayals of women in film helps us to see positive images in a different way.

The question of realism is a central debate among feminist film critics. The pros and cons of this debate can shed light on the important interconnections between form and content.

The element of realism

Realism in film can mean many things. Generally a realistic film appears to be true to life, whether it is in the form of documentary or fiction. Filmmakers use many strategies and conventions to make their films appear life-like. Some viewers find black and white films more realistic than those in colour. Others suggest that if it is easy to relate to characters or situations in a film, this means the film carries a sense of "striking reality". Some feel that a serious or emotionally painful film is more realistic than a comedy, for instance. Some technical qualities — the combination of sound, moving images, and editing — make a film seem inherently realistic.

Realism as an approach to filmmaking is so common that audiences do not often question the techniques used to create its appearance; in fact audiences expect them. Realism in fiction is associated with the tradition of story-telling, where there is an assumption that one action or event will lead to the next, and there will be a beginning, middle, and end that follow a plausible sequence. Yet this style did not drift from the world of lived experience to the world of cinematic imagination; it had to be invented. Film as the "mirror of reality" is more like the mirror in "Alice in Wonderland". Alice did not just look at her reflection, but went through the looking glass into another world, a world of wonder, where not only was everything presented in reverse but her senses were also altered and heightened.*

Realism is a style that does not call attention to itself. Viewers usually respond as if the character's motives were real, when in fact the motivation is usually the creation of a scriptwriter or director. Stories unfold through carefully paced sequences edited to control our excitement and perceptions. Techniques such as long shots inter-cut with close-ups provide the impression that we're getting to know how the characters feel and why they act in a particular way.

Documentary is often considered to be more realistic than fiction film. In the first place realism in documentary films is different: It usually doesn't involve the work of actors and the use of contrived sets. Yet documentary filmmakers also build stories and *selectively* follow events. Just as in fiction film, the use of synchronized sound and careful editing influence viewers' perceptions of and responses to the lives portrayed on the screen.

Many women choose a realistic approach in their filmmaking because such an approach encourages their viewers to identify closely and immediately with characters and situations — to put themselves in the character's shoes — thus creating a new awareness of women's concerns. The more successful films portray strong, interesting women characters who propel the stories forward. Filmmakers know that audiences can follow stories easily and that stories give viewers the opportunity to explore characters in a popular and marketable form.

In Canada, the impact of the women's movement encouraged the government-sponsored National Film Board to set up a women's studio, Studio D, in 1974. Studio D has produced documentaries that use a realist approach, and it provides a unique and important forum for women's perspectives. It also offers women practical training in filmmaking and the opportunity to develop and express themselves through film. Studio D has evaluated the effectiveness of its programs

---

* See Steve Feltes, *Contemporary Films Mini Course on Film Study: A Teacher's Guide* (New York: McGraw Hill, 1973).

Bonnie Klein and Kate Millett from Not a Love Story

through workshops and screenings, and helped define priority areas for new films. Studio D productions include Terri Nash's *If You Love This Planet* about the nuclear arms race; Bonnie Sherr Klein's controversial *Not A Love Story* about pornography; Gail Singer's *Abortion: Stories from North and South*; and *Speaking Our Peace,* a film co-directed by Nash and Klein, about women and peace.

Some of the most vibrant examples of women's realist films come from independent filmmakers. Québecoise Louise Carré's feature *It Can't Be Winter, We Haven't Had Summer Yet* is one example. It is the story of fifty-seven-year-old Adele who, after becoming despondent upon the death of her husband, breaks out of her isolation and rediscovers friendship. With a new sense of self and a zest for life, she ventures off to explore herself and her world. The film's sensitivity and rich character portrayal bring a new vitality and complexity to the common stereotypes of middle-aged women.

There are also exciting, shorter, independently-produced realist documentaries. Canadian Laura Sky's film *Good Monday Morning* is a descriptive, open-ended film that follows a waged worker and

From Good Monday Morning *by Laura Sky*

mother to her job. It examines the problems of office workers, specifically focusing on the implications of new technology. Women workers identify easily with its characters and situations, and women can use the film as a starting point to discuss their own experiences.

The case against realism

Some feminist film critics argue strongly against realism in films. B. Ruby Rich clearly expresses the emotion behind this argument when she writes, "Extolling realism to women is rather like praising the criminal to the victim, so thoroughly have women been falsified under its banner."*

This argument centres on the knowledge that traditional, realist documentaries and Hollywood fiction films have repeatedly offered women images of themselves that do *not* adequately depict the complex realities of their lives. Moreover, these films present images as if

---

* "In the Name of Feminist Film Criticism," *JUMP CUT: Hollywood, Politics and Counter-Cinema,* ed. Peter Steven (Toronto: Between The Lines, 1985) p. 225.

they were a slice of reality — not the working imagination of writers, directors, set designers, actors, and editors.

Both fiction and documentary films use subjects, camera angles and editing in ways that encourage us to think we are seeing reality and truth. They supposedly put women on the screen in a neutral way. But some agree with feminist film critic Eileen McGarry who suggests, "People who are real will be judged according to how they do or don't measure up to current codes" of beauty. McGarry cites Frederick Wiseman's documentary *High School*, in which "The older female teachers, those with glasses, sharp voices, strong regional accents, heavy figures are generally interpreted as less interesting, less sympathetic, in a way less human than those younger women teachers in more modern clothes with more regular facial features."* Again, women are turned into stereotypes.

Some critics say that because a realist approach encourages viewers to identify with characters and situations, it also encourages passive viewing. They strongly believe that it is the role of women filmmakers to use film forms that make viewers remember they are watching a *film*, an interpretation of life, rather than an accurate picture of life itself. They advocate film forms that actively engage the viewer with the filmmaker's ideas and challenge them to interact with the ideas, characters, or situations on the screen. In general, this school of criticism believes feminist content alone does not make a feminist film and that traditional realism inhibits the communication of feminist ideas.

Women filmmakers who have consciously made a break from cinematic realism and experimented with the relationship between film form and feminist ideas have made important contributions to women's filmmaking. Chantal Ackerman's film *Jeanne Dielman* is the fictional story of three days in the life of a women who works as both housekeeper and prostitute and who ends up killing a man. Ackerman's experimental style includes keeping the camera at a distance from the characters and having the camera run for a long time without breaking up the scene. In placing the camera at a distance from the characters, Ackerman gives the viewer time to speculate on the relationship between Jeanne and her environment. She also places the camera low, at her own height, arguing that any other angle

MUSEUM OF MODERN ART

Chantal Ackerman

* McGarry, Eileen, "Documentary Realism & Women's Cinema" in *Women and Film*, Vol. 2, No. 7, 1975.

would be manipulative and would not show her own point of view. The film emphasizes daily details and ordinary gestures with a lengthy precision unusual in fiction films.

Chantal Ackerman comments on one purpose in making *Jeanne Dielman*:

> In the movies the most important images, the most effective and powerful ones are crimes, car chases, etc. Not a woman shown from the back doing dishes. But if it's shown at the same level as the murder.... In fact I think it's much more dramatic. I really think that when she bangs the glass of milk on the table and you think it might spill, that's as dramatic as the murder.*

It is making the ordinary extraordinary, in combination with a personal style of filmmaking that gives Chantal Ackerman a prominent place in feminist filmmaking — despite the fact that she does not accept the label of feminist filmmaker.

Since the mid-1970s, many feminist filmmakers have tended to combine realist and anti-realist approaches in their work. Without denying the value of creating a sense of involvement with the characters, women filmmakers have used a range of techniques to encourage viewers to step back and analyse a film's ideas. These techniques include:

- Stopping the action to introduce political commentary or written words on the screen (inter-titles);
- Moving from a clear storyline into the realm of supernatural or mystical fantasies;
- Introducing the presence of the filmmaker who gives directions and asks questions, or showing film equipment within the film, or having the film's subjects acknowledge that they are being filmed;
- Incorporating fictionalized dramatizations into documentary films and documentary sequences or news-clips into fiction films.

Lizzie Borden, for instance, is one fiction filmmaker who has made amendments to chronological, easy-to-follow plot lines without completely departing from a realist approach. She developed the script

---

* *Other Cinema* Catalogue, London, England 1979.

From Born in Flames *by Lizzie Borden*

for *Born in Flames* in collaboration with the women who act in the film. The movie is a feminist fantasy that presents a group of women who, when confronted with the very ordinary oppression women have experienced for centuries, become armed fighters against the government. The film, set ten years after a social-democratic revolution in the United States, is not traditional "science fiction". The plot is disjunctive, with scenes cutting back and forth between women who represent conflicting positions.*

In Quebec, a number of women filmmakers have experimented with a style that mixes traditional documentary with fiction. Helen Doyle and Nicole Giguère use this technique effectively in their film *This Isn't Wonderland*, an exploration of women and madness. By intercutting dramatic sequences from "Alice in Wonderland" and interviews with women who have confronted madness, as well as with social workers and psychiatrists, the filmmakers illustrate the difficulties and tensions that women encounter in dealing with severe depression.

---

* See the interview with Lizzie Borden, *Heresies*, Vol. 4, No. 14, Issue 16, New York, p. 12.

From This Isn't Wonderland *directed by Helen Doyle and Nicole Guiguère*

Different cultures, different films

Developing a women's culture that adequately reflects and helps to guide political movements is one goal of women filmmakers. But the approaches to this goal vary. In general, a woman might choose to fight for reforms to the present system, she might try to change structures from the inside, or she might work to get rid of the system altogether. It all depends on her political viewpoint. Similarly, women filmmakers are not a homogeneous group and their productions reveal different artistic and political strategies, based on cultural and historical roots.

The problem is, films often sweep us off our feet with their immediacy and excitement, and audiences do not always dissect them to discover their specific political perspectives. The examples below, though cursory, indicate the trends in four widely differing cultural and political climates.

1. Quebec

Quebec women filmmakers are known for their concentration on fiction and frequently experiment with new techniques and ways of expressing their ideas. Although influenced by North American

From La Femme de L'Hôtel *by Lea Poole*

feminism, their work stands apart from the tradition of English Canadian filmmaking because of the direct influence of Quebec nationalism and the struggle to maintain and build a unique culture and language.

La Femme de L'Hôtel, an award-winning film by Québecoise filmmaker Lea Poole, is a mysterious fiction revolving around three women: Andrea, a young woman who is directing her first film; an unnamed woman who plays the central character; and Estelle, a woman Andrea encounters in the hotel who has no history or identity. The film explores women's space, identity, and relationships in a style that creates an unusual shift in understanding of the characters.*

2. Latin America

Despite the enormous obstacles Latin American women face in gaining access to financial and technical resources, they have produced

---

*Brenda Longfellow, *Canadian Forum*, February 1984.

powerful films on such social issues as poverty, housing, and nutrition. They have produced revolutionary underground newsreels in countries where political repression restricts their activity, and made experimental film features in countries such as Cuba and Nicaragua, which encourage the development of indigenous cinema.

In Colombia, a women's filmmaking group, Cine Mujer, has produced films that focus on women, such as *Carmen Carrascal*, an intimate portrait of a rural woman basketweaver. Another Colombian woman, Marta Rodriguez, took an anthropological approach in creating *The Brickmakers*, (co-produced and -directed by Jorge Silva) a sensitive, somewhat surreal documentary on the hardships of a family of brickmakers in her country. Its slow and eerie quality echoes the difficulty of the brickmakers' situation. This powerful documentary provided the impetus for the formation of a union of brickmakers in Colombia.*

From The Brickmakers *by Marta Rodriguez and Jorge Silva*

3. England

In England, a style of feminist experimental filmmaking has been strongly influenced by social and artistic theory — feminism, psychoanalysis, and Marxism, as well as the theatre of Bertolt Brecht and film theory of Jean-Luc Godard. This style seeks to make viewers aware that they are watching a film, and so tries to distance the viewers rather than draw them into the storyline.

The Gold Diggers, made by an all-women crew under the direction of Sally Potter is:

> a critique and an exploration of the way films traditionally portray and use women, both as characters and viewers. The exploration takes the form of a series of images, strung together by the meandering quests of two women: Celeste, a modern-day clerk-typist, and Ruby [played by Julie Christie], the archetypal screen heroine of the twentieth century, disembodied at last from her usual celluloid backdrop. It's a film to approach with an intellectual curiosity, and almost narrative-less dream sequence.†

4. The United States

In the early 1970s, some U.S. feminists who had been involved in the civil rights movement began creating documentaries about the fast

---

* See Julianne Burton, "The Camera as Gun: Two Decades of Culture and Resistance in Latin America", *Latin American Perspectives*, Vol. 5, No. 1, Winter 1978.

† Valerie Schloredt, *Woman Sound*, London, England, June 1984.

From The GoldDiggers *by Sally Potter*

growing women's movement. These films let women speak for themselves and did not concentrate on technical accomplishments, but provided powerful testimony of women's experiences.

We Will Not Be Beaten, originally produced in video by Mary Tiseo and Carol Greenwald, is an intimate look at the difficulties women face when they've been battered and try to break out of the situations, and how transition houses have helped them. Its strength lies in its honesty and ability to discuss openly the women's fears and contradictions.

Many women documentary makers in the United States came to the women's movement from the anti-war and civil rights movements of the 1960s, or were at least strongly influenced by radical filmmaking of that time. In Canada the social-realist style of the National Film Board's John Grierson was one of the biggest influences on documentary production.

Radical films in the United States and Canada throughout the 1960s documented the struggles of people who rarely had a voice in society. They carried a strong, direct message. Similarly, women involved in the new wave of the women's movement also had a message to deliver.

**Documentaries
and the
women's
movement**

91

From We Will Not Be Beaten *by Mary Tiseo and Carol Greenwald*

Getting the message across became easier with the introduction of new technology in the form of lightweight cameras and sound recording equipment developed in the 1950s and 1960s. This technology allowed documentary filmmakers to be less obtrusive while filming; the equipment — lighter, cheaper, and more accessible — was also more easily handled.

Previously, documentary film often separated the sound from the visuals, with voice-over narration playing a major role. In the 1950s and 1960s, a new observational style (better known in North America as "cinéma verité") emerged. This involved recording events as they unfolded and letting the "subjects" speak at length, giving a voice to everyday events and ordinary people.

Women documentary filmmakers have borrowed from cinema verité, adding a few new twists. They usually do not pretend to be outside observers. While news reporters and others who claim objectivity consistently sensationalize, trivialize, or ignore women's issues, filmmakers passionately committed to women's issues are recording the process of their own and their sisters' struggles, carefully and creatively documenting the movement for liberation.

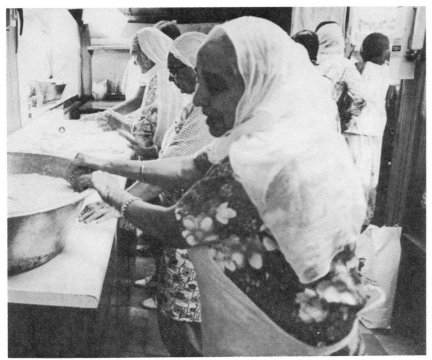

From Emigranté *by Moira Simpson*

Some Features of Feminist Documentaries

- Biographies and autobiographies; women telling their own stories.
- An interest in group or collective relations.
- Less emphasis on "experts"; more on valuing women's own experiences.
- Little or no narration; when narration is used, it is usually delivered by a woman, sometimes a participant in the film.
- Ordinary details of women's lives documented.
- Portrayals of women who are not usually given a voice; for example, working-class women, women of colour, rural women.
- Trust between filmmaker and subject.
- Collective or collaborative working styles.

93

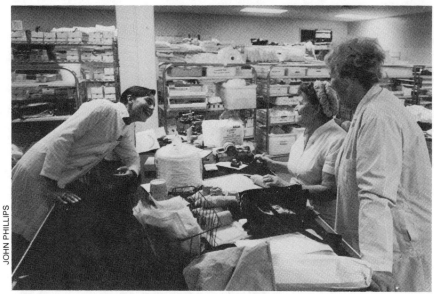

From the making of Yes We Can *by Laura Sky*

Women's documentaries: New images, new insights

Few feminist film critics would argue that all films by feminists are effective in form and content. It is clear that some films are more powerful and better reflect women's experiences, more adequately explore the issues, than others. Yet it is through experimentation that we create new images, new ways of seeing. Together, experimentation and the political purposes embraced by feminists open the way to new insights into social situations, issues, and solutions.

A tack many feminist films take is to show several women talking about their own experiences. In doing this, as film critic Julia Lesage points out, the films of the 1970s took on a structure similar to the political organization of the women's movement: the consciousness-raising sessions that valued experience, stressed process, and focused on issues from women's points of view.* These films have not only been of interest to women who have similar experiences, but they have also offered new insights into personal and collective solutions and stimulated action in their audiences.

---

*Julia Lesage, "Political Aesthetics of Feminist Documentary", *Quarterly Review of Film Studies*, Fall 1978.

As a result of this emphasis, women's documentaries have sometimes been accused of consisting only of "talking heads", in that they largely show individual people talking to the camera. Although there is no denying that this style can be boring, it is also true that hearing women tell their stories can be emotionally stirring. It can provide important support and affirmation for other women.

Some women who produce documentaries choose to portray the extraordinary and well-known women in society as a way of reclaiming women's history and honouring women leaders. We need films about strong women in history, although famous women are sometimes presented as heroines, with achievements we may feel we could never equal. When a subject is removed from their historical, economic, and cultural context, it can be a misrepresentation, isolating them from the community and time in which they lived. If a filmmaker portrays women who do not believe in women's rights as spokespersons for women's issues (such as Mila Mulroney or Nancy Reagan), then the concerns of the majority of women are not being voiced. On the other hand, films that explore "everywoman's" experience, either singly or in groups, can make heroines of us all, and give an important collective spirit to the women's movement. But if we suspend criticism and challenges in order to simply validate each other's experiences, we risk entrenching ourselves in the status quo. Hearing continuous stories of oppression can lead viewers to think of all women as victims. A film on rape victims can often create more fear than anything else. This overwhelming feeling can be overcome if it is put in the context of women organizing to take control over their lives, for example, through forming or becoming involved with a rape crisis centre.

The enthusiasm and dedication of women making movies sometimes outweighs their technical ability. Although some films are out of focus and poorly lit, they are far from unuseable. They speak to and for women and were made despite the ongoing financial and technical discouragement women encounter in the filmmaking industry. As well, the so-called problem of quality has sometimes led women to break new ground in filmmaking just by giving space to those images that may be hard to watch and that have been considered visually uninteresting or disorienting. Women filmmakers are now actively challenging the notions that technical expertise, access to resources, and the right to define what is considered "visually interesting" are the domain of men alone.

SOPHIE BISSONNETTE

From Quel Numero, What Number?

95

Making films about women's experiences can mean making a kitchen, laundry room, or bathroom visually interesting. To start with, getting a 16mm camera, sound equipment, and lights into these poorly lit, small spaces requires ingenuity and creativity that of necessity leads to experimentation. Joyce Rock and Sophie Bissonnette describe their experience filming the wives of Sudbury miners in *A Wives' Tale*:

> It's difficult (impossible) to take 'pretty pictures' under these conditions; their kitchens are small and don't suit well to the movements of a film crew; children scream and cry into the microphone making it hard to hear. The dramatic moments of their lives don't often happen in public and even more rarely under the insistent gaze of the camera.*

In other words, women's films demand viewers with open eyes and open minds — audiences ready to look for something completely different.

The debates and controversies will continue — over form and content, the roles of realism and experimentation, the need for certain goals and special challenges. In the end we can certainly find no succinct definition of feminist filmmaking that will work for everybody. The most important thing for us is that film users participate actively in the debate — not just by watching films and videos, but by looking at them critically, by talking about them, by getting others to see them.

The results of this new, engaged activity will benefit us all. The work will contribute to a growing confidence in women's culture and history. It will encourage new and sustained work by women exploring issues, problems, and solutions important to other women today. After all, the greater and more varied the use of women's films and videos, the greater will be the opportunities for transforming new images into new action.

*Interview with the filmmakers, *DEC Films Catalogue*, Toronto, 1982.

The history of women in the cinema is a long and rich one. However, it is a difficult landscape to map. Women have been in front of the cameras, acting on the screen, as well as watching in the audience. They've also worked behind the screen, as well as watching in the audience. They've also worked behind the scenes in traditional roles, as makeup artists and sometimes winning awards for costume making and design. But women have also written, directed, and produced films, done camera work, sound, and lighting right from the beginning of film as an art form and as an industry. Women have also distributed films, exhibited them, and written about them. The silence of history books blocks out these achievements.

Women's history in film is only now being rediscovered, reconstructed, studied, and written. What follows highlights a few landmarks or departure points in women's cinema history.

Women in film history: Some landmarks

*This section was written by Susan Ditta, who is a freelance arts administrator and film and video programmer, living in Toronto and Peterborough, Ontario.

* Sources for the information in this section include Marjorie Rosen, *Popcorn Venus* (New York: Avon, 1974); Barbara Martineau-Halpern (a.k.a. Sara Halprin), "Leading Ladies Behind the Camera," *Cinema Canada*, No. 71, Jan.-Feb. 1981; Kay Armitage and Linda Beath, *Notes in Women in Film Catalogue*, 1973, Toronto.

In France in the 1890s:

Alice Guy may have been the first woman filmmaker. She was certainly the first woman to direct fiction films; in fact . . .

In 1896:

Alice Guy developed the techniques for fictional filmmaking while the Lumière brothers of France were recording actual events and . . .

In 1910:

She formed her own production company and was quoted as saying "women can do all the things connected with film as easily as a man."

Nell Shipman in Back to God's Country

In Canada:

Nell Shipman produced and often starred in a series of successful features, did her own stunts, wrote scripts, photographed and produced.

Nell wrote the script, played the lead role, and was the main creative force behind the classic melodrama, *Back to God's Country*.

MUSEUM OF MODERN ART FILM STILL ARCHIVES

The Fall of the Romanov Dynasty *by Esther Shub*

Esther Shub created the first compilation film, *The Fall of the Romanov Dynasty*, in 1927.

The Brumberg sisters were widely recognized as Russia's premiere animators.

Jacqueline Audry began her film career in 1933 and produced one of the first feminist films in 1943. She produced seventeen features in which the women characters were central. Her films often criticized society's attempts to restrict and define female behaviour.

Germaine Dulac was one of France's first feminist filmmakers. She made twenty-three films in the 1920s and 1930s, founded film societies, and was active in the unionization of film industry workers.

From Germaine Dulac's 'The Smiling Madame Beudet'

Speaking of animation:

Women have been widely recognized for originating and evolving animation. In the 1920s, German filmmaker Lotte Reiniger made the first full-length animated film in the world, *The Adventures of Prince Achmed*, using shadow puppets. In the 1930s, Mary Ellen Bute experimented with abstract forms of animation in the United States. Many female animators have won international acclaim for their work, including Canadians Evelyn Lambert, Alma Duncan, and Babs McLaren; and Veronika Stoul and Caroline Leaf from the United States.

Lotte Reiniger

From Nina Polanski *by Lotte Reiniger*

Evelyn Lambert

The making of the film The Hoarder *by Evelyn Lambert*

Animation was considered 'women's work'. It required patience, a delicate touch, and did not call for large casts and crews. Women filmmakers faced many of the prejudices of women workers in any industry. Were they serious enough, aggressive, and ambitious? Could they show the leadership required to manage a big production?

Women also faced traditional resistance and had to overcome attitudes that said they could not handle the technical and physical side of the industry. They could produce, but could they shoot, do sound, edit, or handle lights?

Women have been on the cutting edge, and made crucial contributions in the early stages of various film movements. In Germany, Lotte Reiniger invented frame by frame filmmaking using silhouette figures. Maya Deren was one of the first filmmakers in the United States to make use of 16mm film in the 1940s. Her work as an independent filmmaker fostered the New American Cinema Movement.

But:

Can she lift the camera?

Nevertheless:

101

In the late 1940s and 1950s:

Frances Marion

Before Hollywood became home to a powerful elite, it was hungry for talent — talent that women provided. Lois Weber, Frances Marion, and Anita Loos were all major forces in the feature film industry. However, after the Second World War, there was a push to keep women in front of the cameras, on the screen. Women making films in Hollywood during the late 1940s and 1950s often used pseudonyms, left their names off the credits or gave directing credit to their husbands.

In fact:

Large numbers of women have been silent partners in the production of films or were credited as being production secretaries when they did the work of a male producer.

At the National Film Board:

Gudrun Parker

Evelyn Spice Cherry, Margaret Perry, Judith Crawley, Gudrun Parker, Jane Marsh, and many other women worked on wartime documentaries in several capacities. After the war, many of these women were forgotten and their role in documentary production was severely reduced.

Until the 1960s when:

A changing political climate prompted another metamorphosis for women in filmmaking. Beryl Fox and Dodi Robb became key players in the production of films for Canadian television. The *Challenge for Change* series at the Film Board provided a vehicle for women such as

Bonnie Sherr Klein, Dorothy Henaut, and Kathleen Shannon. Series such as *Working Mothers* showed women not as isolated heroines, but as real people engaged in daily struggles.

In the late 1960s and 1970s:

From La Vie Revée (Dream Life) *by Mireille Dansereau*

There was a resurgence of women behind the cameras in all aspects of film production. Lina Wertmuller, Marguerite Duras, Elaine May, Nellie Kaplan, and Go Be Se all produced big-budget feature films. Karen Sperling, Barbara Loden, and Mireille Dansereau made a number of low-budget films.

Marguerite Duras

New wave movements:

Agnes Varda

Agnes Varda and Véra Chytilová were prominent in the French and Czechoslovakian new wave film movements. Many feminist filmmakers have developed new forms and new structures because the old ones simply were not appropriate. Many women have also demonstrated a new style of directing and a different way of working with casts and crews.

Studio D:

The founding in 1974 of a women's studio at the National Film Board provided a unique opportunity for women to make films from their own perspective about the issues that concerned them. Award-winning productions such as *Not A Love Story* and *If You Love This Planet* created a high profile for the women who worked on them. But the films and filmmakers have sometimes suffered from the institutionalization of government funded organizations.

NFB

National Film Board, Studio D directors, Bonnie Klein and Terri Nash

Women have carved new ground in independent production in Canada. Alternative cinema has grown with the work of Patricia Gruben, Judith Doyle, Sophie Bissonnette, Mo Simpson, Holly Dale, Janis Cole, Jackie Levitin, Mary Jane Gomes, and dozens of others who have criss-crossed the boundaries of conventional genres, movements, and methods of working.

Film co-operatives are groups of independent filmmakers who provide each other with artistic and technical support. The co-op movement in English Canada is only about ten years old, but it has inspired and facilitated the work of women filmmakers from coast to coast, including Peg Campbell of Vancouver and Lulu Keating of Halifax. Co-ops have made it possible for women to produce films outside of major industry centres of Toronto and Montreal.

Independent production:

Film co-ops:

Lists of Distributors of Films on Women's Concerns

To find films on specific issues it is useful to contact as many distributors as possible to get a sense of what is available. Catalogues are usually available on request, although there is often a small charge from distributors.

The following list incorporates French and English language distributors as well as distributors of video and slide-shows (although slide-show distribution is not as well developed). Some distributors listed here have resources on issues of concern to women, but their films are not necessarily produced by women. We've identified the distributors who have special collections of films by women (see the key, below). You can help by letting us know if we've missed anyone.

Key

* French language distributors
● Video distributors (primarily experimental productions)
♀ Distributor with a special catalogue or collection of films by women for women

● Artists' Resource
Centre (ARC)
658 Queen St. W.
Toronto, Ont.
M6J 1E5
(416) 947-9169
— entirely
experimental
collection

● Art Metropole
217 Richmond St. W.
Toronto, Ont.
M5V 1W2
(416) 977-1685
— experimental work
only

* Astral Films
195 Boul. Montpellier
St. Laurent, Que.
H4N 2G5
(514) 748-6976

* Astral Bellevue
Classics
720 King St. W.
Suite 600
Toronto, Ont.
M5V 2T3
(416) 362-1215

* Audiovideothèque/
CISE
Hôpital
Sainte-Justine
3175 chemin de la
Côte-Ste. Catherine
Montreal, Que.
H3T 1C5

Bouchard et Associés
136 rue St. Paul est
Montreal, Que.
H2Y 1G6
(514) 861-0983

British Broadcasting
(BBC) Education and
Training
214 King St. W.
Suite 311
Toronto, Ont.
M5H 1K1
(416) 585-2583

♀ Canadian
Filmmakers
Distribution Centre
(CFMDC)
67A Portland St.
Toronto, Ont.
M5V 2M9
(416) 593-1808
— independent
producers co-op,
emphasizes
experimental

♀ Canadian
Filmmakers
Distribution West
525 West Pender #1
Vancouver, B.C.
V6B 1V5
(604) 684-3014
— independent
producers co-op,
emphasizes
experimental

Canadian Learning
Company
2229 Kingston Road
Suite 203
Scarborough, Ont.
M1N 1T8
(416) 265-3333

* Carrefour
International
4258 Avenue de
Lorimier
Montreal, Que.
H2H 2B1
(514) 527-6611
— independent
producers,
emphasizes Third
World films

* Cimadis Inc.
1564 - A Lajoie
Montreal, Que.
H2V 1R5
(514) 849-9530

* Cine-Contact
826 La Gauchetiere
St. E.
Montreal, Que.
H2L 2N2
(514) 849-9530

* Cinéma Libre
♀ 4872 rue Papineau
Montreal, Que.
H2H 1V6
(514) 526-0473
— independent,
international, and
Quebecois socially
concerned films;
different film styles

Cinephile
173 Willow Ave.
Toronto, Ont.
M4E 3K4
(416) 699-8744
— independent fiction
features

♀ DEC Films
(Development
Education Centre)
229 College St.
Toronto, Ont.
M5T 1R4
(416) 597-0524
— independent,
Canadian and
international,
socially concerned;
documentary and
fiction, films and
videos

Doomsday Studios
1627 Barrington St.
Halifax, N.S. B3J 1Z6
(902) 422-3494

Educfilm Inc.
643 rue Stuart
Montreal, Que.
H2V 3H2
(514) 274-6900

* FILM FILM
3684 Boulevard St.
Laurent
Montreal,Que.
H2X 2V4
(514) 843-4711
— emphasizes
experimental work

* Les Films du
Crepuscule
4503 rue Saint-Denis
Bureau 1
Montreal, Que.
H2J 2L4
(514) 849-2477
— independent
productions

The Funnel
507 King St. East
Toronto, Ont.
M5A 1M3
(416) 364-7003
— experimental work
only

Gordon Watt Films
3241 Kennedy Road
Unit 3
Scarborough, Ont.
M1V 2J8
(416) 291-9321

● Groupe
* D'Intervention Video
♀ 1308 Gilford
Montreal, Que.
H2J 1R5
(514) 524-3259
— independent,
social issues

Health Media
Distributors
629a Mt. Pleasant
Road
Toronto, Ont.
M4S 2M9
(416) 488-7885

Hy Perspectives
Media Group
1164 Hamilton St.
3rd Floor
Vancouver, B.C.
V6B 2S3
(604) 683-2689
— native people

♀ IDERA Films
2524 Cypress St.
Vancouver, B.C.
V6J 3N2
(604) 738-8815
— social issues,
international,
documentary

International
Telefilm Enterprises
47 Densley Ave.
Toronto, Ont.
M6M 5A8
(416) 241-4483
1200 West Pender
#601
Vancouver, B.C.
V6E 2S9
(604) 685-2616

Kinetic Film
Enterprises
781 Gerrard St. E.
Toronto, Ont.
M4M 1Y5
(416) 469-4155

J.A. LaPointe Films
10800 rue Jeanne
Mance
Montreal, Que.
H3L 3C4
— primarily French
language

Magic Lantern Film
Distributors
872 Winston
Churchill Blvd.
Oakville, Ont.
L6J 4Z2
(416) 844-7216

Marlin Motion
Pictures Ltd.
211 Watline Ave.
Suite 200
Mississauga, Ont.
L4Z 1P3

McIntyre
Educational Media
30 Kelfield St.
Rexdale, Ont.
M9W 5A2
(416) 245-7800

Mobius Productions
290 Palmerston Ave.
Toronto, Ont.
M6J 2J3
(416) 964-8484

Modern Talking
Picture Service
143 Sparks Ave.
Willowdale, Ont.
M2H 2S5
(416) 489-7293

Monitor North
515 N. Syndicate
#11
Thunder Bay, Ont.
P7C 3X2
(807) 623-1506

Multimedia
Audiovisual
5225 rue Berri
Montreal, Que.
H2J 2S4
(514) 273-4251

New Cinema
75 Horner Ave.
Toronto, Ont.
M8Z 4X5
(416) 251-3728

Omega Films
70 Milner Ave.
Unit 5A
Scarborough, Ont.
M1S 3P8
(416) 291-4733

Pan Canadian Film
Distributors
20 Queen St. W.
Toronto, Ont.
M5H 3S4
(416) 596-2200

* Parlimage
4572 avenue de
Lorimier
Montreal, Que.
H2H 2B5
(514) 526-4423

* PRIM
3981 Boulevard St.
Laurent Suite 310
Montreal, Que.
H2W 1Y5
(514) 849-5065

PVS Productions
11 Austin Cres.
Toronto, Ont.
M5R 3E4
(416) 535-5860

♀ Skyworks
⚦ 566 Palmerston Ave.
Toronto, Ont.
M6G 2P7
(416) 536-6581
— distributes the
films of Laura Sky

* Spirafilm
56 rue St. Pierre,
Bureau 301
Quebec City, Que.
G1K 4A1
(418) 694-0786

Thomas Howe
Associates
1 - 1226 Homer St.
Vancouver, B.C.
V6B 2Y5
(604) 687-4215

● V/Tape
489 College St.
5th Floor
Toronto, Ont.
M6G 1A5
(416) 925-1961
— also helps with
programming video
tapes, especially
independent
productions

* Video Femmes
♀ 56 St. Pierre #203
⚦ Quebec City, Que.
G1R 4A1
(418) 692-3090
— a production/
distribution group;
both film and video

Video Out
261 Powell St.
Vancouver, B.C.
V6A 1G3
(604) 688-4336

Video Pool
89 Princess St.
2nd Floor
Winnipeg, Man.
R3L 1Y5
(204) 949-9134

* Videographe
4550 Garnier
Montreal, Que.
H2J 3S6
— focus on
independent Quebec
videos; also a
production group

Visual Education
Centre
75 Horner Ave.
Toronto, Ont.
M8Z 4X5
(416) 252-5907

Western Front
303 East 8th Ave.
Vancouver, B.C.
V5G 1S1
(604) 867-9343

♀ Women in Focus
⚦ 456 West Broadway
Suite 204
Vancouver, B.C.
V5Y 1R3
(604) 872-2250
— independent, focus
on Canadian,
international; also
production group

♀ Women's Workshop
⚦ 499 Hibiscus Ave.
London, Ont.
N6H 3P2
(519) 472-1185
— production/
distribution of their
own work

NOTE: There are two general resource books often available in libraries, audio-visual departments of universities, colleges, and school boards which provide helpful information for locating films and videos distributed in Canada. They are updated periodically so the addresses of distributors should be accurate.

1) CFFS (Canadian Federation of Film Societies) INDEX of 16mm and 35mm feature length films with production and distribution details.

P.O. Box 484
Station A
Toronto, Ont. M5W 1E4
(approximately $20.)

2) Canadian Film Digest Yearbook — Information on the film industry including sections on distribution, exhibition, production, government film agencies.

175 Bloor Street East
Toronto, Ont. M4W 1E1
(approximately $20.)

Independent Film Co-operatives — Production/Distribution

Independent filmmakers' production co-operatives often distribute their own resources. A film co-operative in your region may help you find local women filmmakers. There is an umbrella organization for independent filmmakers. Although not a distribution group, it can help with general information on film co-operatives and independent filmmakers.

Independent Film and Video Alliance
Box 545
P.O. Desjardins
Montreal, Que. H5B 1B6
(514) 521-0569

The following are production co-ops. Some distribute their own films.

Atlantic Filmmakers'
Co-op
1588 Barrington St.
Halifax, N.S. B3J 1Z6
(902) 423-8833

Calgary Society of
Independent
Filmmakers
P.O. Box 30089
Station B
Calgary, Alta. T3M 4N7
(403) 277-1741

Cineworks
525 West Pender St.
Vancouver, B.C.
V6B 1V9
(604) 685-3841

Cooperative Des
Artisans Du Cinéma
En Maravie
C.P. 460
Edmunston, N.B.
E3V 3L1
(516) 739-7458

Femmes en Focus
C.P. 865
Petit Rocher, N.B.
(506) 783-8434

Island Media Arts
Co-op
P.O. Box 2726
Charlottetown, P.E.I.
C1A 8C3
(902) 892-3790

Liaison of Independent
Filmmakers of Toronto
101 Niagara St.
Suite 304
Toronto, Ont.
(416) 596-8233

MAIN Film
4060 Saint-Laurent
Suite 303
Montreal, Que.
H2W 1Y9
(514) 845-7442

New Brunswick
Filmmakers' Coop
P.O. Box 1537
Fredericton, N.B.
E3B 3N4
(506) 455-1632

Newfoundland
Independent
Filmmakers Co-op
(NIFCO)
P.O. Box 9116
Station B
St. John's, Nfld.
A1A 2X3
(709) 753-6121

Saskatchewan
Filmpool
2108 Rae St.
Regina, Sask. S4T 2E7
(306) 527-8818

Winnipeg Film Group
99 Adelaide St.
Winnipeg, Man.
R3A 0W2
(204) 942-6795

A Note on Women's Production Groups

An increasing number of independent women media producers are forming production groups. These groups do not necessarily distribute the resources that they produce, but they are interested in meeting women to talk about their films, videos, or slide-shows and the issues they raise. These media groups add important energy to women's culture in Canada. Often they can be located through a film co-operative, an independent distributor, or a National Film Board office.

Free Films at the Public Library

Many libraries offer good selections of women's films as well as information on available films for programming purposes. Usually film collections are located in big city libraries, but smaller libraries will often borrow films for you through the regional networks. If your library doesn't have an in-house collection, ask to borrow resources through another library in the area. Catalogues are usually available. You can also ask a library to purchase a particular film. Libraries are there to service and support community needs. They appreciate letters or phone calls that indicate resources individuals and groups in the community would use.

There is no charge for use of library resources, and some libraries lend out equipment as well. However, libraries do not have the rights to allow you to charge an entrance fee for their film; for fundraisers, it is therefore necessary to go directly to the distributor. Nor do libraries have the rights to lend films to people for use within institutions, such as government bodies or universities.

Women's Centres/Resource Centres

Despite restricted budgets, some women's centres have a few films that they may lend for a service fee, or for free.

There are also a number of learner centres and cross-cultural communications centres across Canada. Some of them have films that they lend for a service fee. These centres usually focus on resources about women and development or visible minorities and immigrant women.

Universities/Colleges/School Boards/Government Agencies/ Unions/Churches

If you belong to, or work for, any of these organizations, it's possible that they have audio-visual collections, and some resources that would be of specific interest to women. They must be used for events

associated with the institution, and community groups cannot usually borrow films for public use from them. But for previewing purposes, audio-visual collections within educational institutions, unions, and churches are sometimes available on request. The larger collections of audio-visual material are usually catalogued by universities, school boards, government agencies, or the central locations of unions or churches.

National Film Board (NFB)

The NFB has film libraries across the country. Their films are available free but you cannot charge an entrance fee when showing them. If you do want to charge (for a fundraiser, for example), you will have to negotiate a contract and price with the NFB. Many of the films of interest to women's groups are produced by Studio D: the Women's Studio of the NFB. You can request specific information about their productions.

Studio D
National Film Board
P.O. Box 6100
Station A
Montreal, Quebec
H3C 3H5
(514) 283-9000

Atlantic Region:

Regional Office
1572 Barrington St.
Halifax, N.S. B3J 1Z6
Office: (902) 426-6000
Film Library:
(902) 426-6001

Sydney Shopping Mall
Prince Street
Sydney, N.S.
B1P 5K8
(902) 564-7770

Terminal Plaza
Building
1222 Main Street
Moncton, N.B. E1C 1H6
(506) 388-6101

7 Market Square
Saint John, N. B.
E2L 1E7
(506) 648-4996

202 Richmond St.
Charlottetown, P.E.I.
C1A 1J2
(902) 892-6612

Building 255
Pleasantville
St. John's, Nfld.
A1A 1N3
(709) 772-5005

10 Main St.
Corner Brook, Nfld.
A2H 1C1
(709) 634-4295

Quebec Region:

Regional Office
Complexe Guy-Favreau
200 Dorchester
Blvd. W.
East Tower, Ste. 102
Montreal, Que.
H2Z 1X4
(514) 283-4823

72 Cartier St. W.
Chicoutimi, Que.
G7J 1G2
(418) 543-0711

350, rue St Joseph Est
Quebec City, Que.
G1K 3B2
Office: (418) 694-3176
Film Library:
(418) 694-3852

124 Vimy St.
Rimouski, Que.
G5L 3J6
Office: (418) 722-3088
Film Library:
(418) 722-3086

315 King St. W. Ste. 3
Sherbrooke, Que.
J1H 1R2
Office: (819) 565-4915
Film Library
(819) 565-4931

Room 502, Pollack
Building
140 St. Antoine St.
Trois Rivières, Que.
G9A 5N6
Office: (819) 375-5714
Film Library:
(819) 375-5811

42 Mgr Rhéaume East
Rouyn, Que. J9X 3J5
(819) 762-6051

Ontario Region:

Regional Office
Mackenzie Building
1 Lombard St.
Toronto, Ont. M5C 1J6
Office: (416) 973-9094
Film Library:
(416) 973-9093

First Place Hamilton
10 West Ave. S.
Hamilton, Ontario
L8N 3Y8
(416) 523-2347

New Federal Building
Clarence Street
Kingston, Ont.
K7L 1X0
Office: (613) 547-2470
Film Library:
(613) 547-2471

Suite 207
659 King St. E.
Kitchener, Ont.
N2G 2M4
Office: (519) 743-2771
Film Library:
(519) 743-4661

366 Oxford St. E.
London, Ont. N6A 1V7
(519) 679-4120

195 First Ave. W.
North Bay, Ont.
P1B 3B8
(705) 472-4740

910 Victoria Ave.
Thunder Bay, Ont.
P7C 1B4
(807) 623-5224

National Capital:

150 Kent St., Suite 642
Ottawa, Ont. K1A 0M9
Office: (613) 996-4863
Film Library:
(613) 996-4861

Prairie Region:

Regional Office
245 Main St.
Winnipeg, Man.
R3C 1A7
Office: (204) 949-4129
Film Library:
(204) 949-4131

222 1st St. S. E.
P.O. Box 2959,
Station M
Calgary, Alta. T2P 3C3
Office: (403) 231-5338
Film Library:
(403) 231-5414

Centennial Building
10031 - 103rd Ave.
Edmonton. Alta.
T5J 0G9
Office: (403) 420-3012
Film Library:
(403) 420-3010

Suite 111
2001 Cornwall St.
Regina, Sask. S4P 2K6
Office: (306) 359-5011
Film Library:
(306) 359-5014

424 - 21st St. E.
Saskatoon, Sask.
S7K 0C2
Office: (306) 665-4246
Film Library:
(306) 665-4245

Pacific Region:

Regional Office
1161 W. Georgia St.
Vancouver, B.C.
V6E 3G4
Office: (604) 666-1718
Film Library:
(604) 666-1716

545 Quebec St.
Prince George, B.C.
V2L 1W6
(604) 564-5657

811 Wharf St.
Victoria, B.C. V8W 1T2
Office: (604) 388-3869
Film Library:
(604) 388-3868

International Resources

The following list is incomplete. We've included only some of the well known international independent distributors of women's films. They are listed to help anyone interested in researching or programming films that are not presently available in Canada. We have mainly listed English language distributors.

United States Distributors

Black Filmmaker
Distribution Service
P.O. Box 315, Franklin
Lakes, N.J. 07417

Cinema Guild
1695 Broadway, Ste.
802
New York, New York
10019
(212) 246-5522

First Run Features
153 Waverly Pl.
New York, New York
10014
(212) 243-0600

Goddess Films
(films of Barbara
Hammer)
129 W. 22nd St.
New York, New York
10011
(212) 675-4740

Icarus Films
200 Park Ave. S., Rm.
1319
New York, New York
10013
(212) 674-3375

Iris Video
P.O. Box 7133
Powderhorn Station
Minneapolis,
Minnesota 55407

Media Network
Information Center
208 W. 13th St.
New York, New York
10011
(212) 620-0877
— information on
finding films; first
request is free

New Day Films
22 Riverview Dr.
Wayne, N. J. 07470
(201) 633-0212

Pandora Films
1697 Broadway, Rm.
1109
New York, New York
10019

Third World Newsreel
335 W. 38th St., 5th
Flr.,
New York, New York
10018
(212) 947-9277

Women Make Movies
225 Lafayette St., Rm.
212
New York, New York,
10012

British Distributors

Cinema of Women
27 Clerkenwell Close
London, England EC1R
0AT

Circles (a distribution
network)
113 Roman Road
London, England E2 OHV

The Other Cinema
79 Wardour St.
London, England
W1V 3TH

South Wales Women's
Film Co-op
Chapter Arts Centre
Cardiff, South Wales

Australian Distributors

Sydney Filmmakers'
Co-op
P.O. Box 217
Kings Cross, New
South Wales 2011
Australia

Colombia, South America

Cine Mujer
Apartado Aereo 2758
Bogota, Colombia

The Netherlands

Cinemien
Amstel 256A
1017 AL
Amsterdam, The
Netherlands
Tel: 31-20-279501

Cineographies

Publications of Available Audio-Visuals on Women's Issues

NOTE: This list complements the women's films catalogues noted in the section on distributors.

Canada

Beyond the Image: A guide to films about women and change, by National Film Board of Canada (2nd edition) P.O. Box 6100, Montreal, Que. H3C 3H5 Canada 1984; Selected annotated lists of films on a variety of social issues, includes resources by independent distributors as well as NFB; free.

Audio-visual Resources on Sexuality, Planned Parenthood Federation of Canada, 1984, #200 - 151 Slater St., Ottawa, Ont. K1P 5H3; selected annotated list on audio-visuals relating to sexuality.

Filmography, Ontario Ministry of Labour, Women's Bureau, 400 University Ave., Toronto, Ont. M7A 1T7; resources on women and work, free for use in Ontario.

Filmography, Public Service Commission of Canada, West Tower, Esplanade Laurier, Ottawa, Ont. K1A 0M7; filmography free from Resource Centre, Office of Equal Opportunities, Ottawa, Ont.

Resources for Feminist Research, 252 Bloor St. W., Toronto, Ont. M5S 1V6; filmographies within particular issues of the periodical, "Women and Agriculture", "Women and Education", "Women and Disability", "The Lesbian Issue".

Women's Resource Catalogue, Women's Program, Secretary of State, Ottawa, Ont.; includes lists of print and audio-visual resources on a range of women's issues, free.

Family Violence Film Catalogue, National Clearing House on Family Violence, Health and Welfare Canada, Ottawa, Ont. K1A 1B4 (613) 995-1050; 200 audio-visual resources on child abuse, sexual abuse and battering, free.

'Women, Work and Unions — A Cineography", Dinah Forbes in *Union Sisters,* pp. 377-96, ed. by Linda Briskin and Lynda Yanz, 1983, Women's Educational Press, 229 College St., Toronto, Ont.; thorough listing of English and French audio-visuals on women's work.

Women's Studies Video Resource Catalogue, TV Ontario Customer Services, Box 200 Station Q, Toronto, Ont. M4T 2T1; productions of TV Ontario, only available in Ontario.

Publications of Films in Distribution in the U.S.

Note: Several annotated lists of audio-visuals on women have been produced in the United States. Many of the films on these lists are available in Canada as well. The following list does not include all cineographies available: it is a selection of the most useful ones.

'Filmographies of Women Directors', in *Sexual Strategems,* by Patricia Erens, New York, Horizon Press, 1979; international listing of films in distribution.

Films By And Or About Women: 1972 Directory of Filmmakers, Films and Distributors, Internationally, Past and Present, by Kaye Sullivan; write Women's History Research Center, 2324 Oak St., Berkeley Cal., 94708.

Past 60: The Older Women in Print and Film, by Carol Hollenshead (1977); Institute of Gerontology, University of Michigan, Wayne State University, 520 East Liberty St., Ann Arbor, Michigan, 48109; over 60 listings, annotated, with distributors.

Positive Images, by Linda Artel and Susan Wengraf, San Francisco, Booklegger Press, 1976; a guide to nonsexist films for young people with subject index, distributors.

Guide to Films on Reproductive Rights, Media Network and the Reproductive Rights National Network, 208 W. 13th St., New York, New York, 10011; a thorough, useful list for activists working on reproductive rights issues.

Reel Change: A Guide to Social Issue Films, the Film Fund, Patricia Pey, Media Network 208 W. 13th St. New York, New York 10011; list of over 500 dramatic features, documentaries, shorts, video-tapes and slideshows.

Women's Films in Print, Bonnie Dawson, Booklegger Press, 555 29th St. San Francisco, California 94131, 1975; an annotated list of 800 films by women.

Images of Color: A Guide to Media From and For Asian, Black, Hispanic and Native American Communities, Media Network and Center for Third World Organizing, 121 Fulton St., 5th Fl., New York, New York, 10038.

Australia
A Catalogue of Independent Women's Films, Sydney Women's Film Group, P.O. Box 217, Kings Cross NSW 2011, Australia; international listings, 1979.

Britain
Women's Film List, British Film Institute, 81 Dean St., London, England, W1V 6AA, 1978.

International
Powerful Images: A Women's Guide to Audiovisual Resources. Isis International, via Santa Maria dell'Anima 30, Rome, 00186 Italy, 1986.

118

Selected Bibliography

Magazines

Fuse; 489 College St., Toronto, Ont. M6G 1A5; a Canadian magazine on art and politics supporting independent production, consistent coverage from feminists.

Heresies: A Feminist Publication on Art and Politics, 611 Broadway, Room 609, New York, 10012; No. 16 is specifically on film and video.

Jump Cut: A Review of Contemporary Media, P.O. Box 865, Berkeley, California, 94701; film reviews and articles on both Hollywood and independent films; consistent coverage of feminist criticism and women's filmmaking.

Videoguide, Satellite, Video Exchange Society, 261 Powell St., Vancouver, B.C. V6A 1G3; consistent material by women on feminist video.

Books

Carrieres, Louise, *Femmes et Cinéma Québecois*, Boréal Express, 5450 Chemin de la Côte-des-Neiges, Bureau 2121, Montreal, Que. H3T 1Y6; in French only, a thorough overview of women and Quebec cinema.

Kaplan, E. Ann, *Women and Film: Both Sides of the Camera*, Methuen, 11 New Fetter Lane, London EC4P 4EE; structured as a women and film course, less difficult than many feminist film theory books.

Steven, Peter, ed., *Jump Cut: Hollywood, Politics and Counter-Cinema*, 1985: Between The Lines, 229 College St., Toronto, Ont. M5T 1R4; includes many *Jump Cut* magazine articles on women's cinema, with a special section on lesbians and film.

On Using Media

Blackaby, Linda with Dan Georgakas and Barbara Margolis, *In Focus: A Guide to Using Films*, New York, 1980; excellent resource

book, practical information on setting up a screening, running a projector, organizing speakers, etc. Available in Canada through DEC Books, 229 College St., Toronto, Ont.

Scheiman, Diane and Stacey Oliker, *The Media Book: Making the Media Work for Your Grassroots Group*, 1981; based on a group experience, it gives practical details on how to work with the press; available from Committee to Defend Reproductive Rights, 1638 Haight St., San Francisco, California 94117.

Printed in Canada